To Become The Sun

Living Metaphors for Trauma, Healing and Spirit

To Become The Sun

Living Metaphors for Trauma, Healing and Spirit

Copyright c. 2018 Ani Rose Whaleswan USA

whalesunpress@gmail.com

All photos and paintings by Ani Rose Whaleswan

(color photos can be seen on the website and Facebook page)

Also self-published by ARW

<u>A Safe Pace for Pearl</u>. Whale dreams and paintings that helped a woman heal, 2017.

<u>We Have Come Far: Gifts of Healing from Survivors of Extreme Abuse</u> 21 author's best advice on healing, 2014.

<u>Unlimited...</u> 18 paintings, 13 poems, and some small thoughts on art and healing, 2012.

You have permission to copy what you want for healing needs, but I would appreciate that you include the book and author reference. Thank you, Ani Rose

This book is dedicated to Sunny,

a young friend who knows

that in the face of it all

everything still shines.

A Very Brief Introduction

"Our age is retrospective. It builds the sepulchers of the fathers. It writes biographies, histories and criticism. The foregoing generations beheld God and nature face to face; we, through their eyes. Why should not we also enjoy an original relation to the universe? Why should not we have poetry and philosophy of insight and not tradition, and a religion by revelation to us, and not by history of theirs? Embosomed for a season in nature, whose floods of life stream around us and through us, and invite us, by the powers they supply, to action proportioned to nature, why should we grope among the bones of the past, or put the living generation into masquerade out of its faded wardrobe. The sun shines today also."

(Ralph Waldo Emerson in <u>Nature,</u> 1836, p 9)

The thoughts I share throughout this book rely heavily upon the ideas in this quote, and I very intentionally apply the concepts to the fields of trauma and healing. Particularly in these days of global turmoil, I would add to Emerson's list and ask, "why should we not have psychology and psychiatry and all the myriad therapies for mind/body and spiritual help (theology), be born and carried through ***an original relationship to the universe***?"

"We are called to assist the earth, to heal her wounds, and in the process, heal our own." Ecologist Wangari Maathai, winner of the 2004 Nobel Peace Prize.

The natural world gives us all the imagery and meaning we need to be mirrored and held empathically, to be challenged, to learn wisdom and resiliency and sustainability for the self and the self as we exist in connection. Without taking away from the supports of psychology and theology, therapists and ministers and activists for the earth, the ideas here are meant to bring them together a bit, to add support, nuance, the power of metaphor and art, some story-telling – all forms of "seeing with new eyes."

If you don't really relate to the words, "trauma, healing and Spirit" then substitute terms that do work for you. Try living metaphors: the language of nature. How about "earthquake, sunrise and breath?"

Metaphor invites us into deep and interwoven meaning. The metaphors here are from nature and they offer new insight in understanding trauma and healing and spirit. One is not supposed to explain metaphor but simply let it work its magic. Therefore, I invite you to simply delve in and see what happens.

Peace and all good,

Ani Rose

Index..page

I am Mountain
    Strong in soft places...13
I am Pearl
    Transformative power..35
I am the Unfolding Flower
    Knowing when to bloom from the inside.......................53
I am Stones
    I witness, honor, connect, resonate..................................73
I am Compost
    Breaking down to provide for new life............................93
I am Humming Bird
    My remarkable power lay in my smallness................109
I am Wave
    The coming and going and the still point between........125
I am Embers
    The things which continue and ignite..........................145
I am Shadow
    Darkness illuminating light illuminating dark..............163
To Become the Sun 183

Why this book?..203
Resources..211

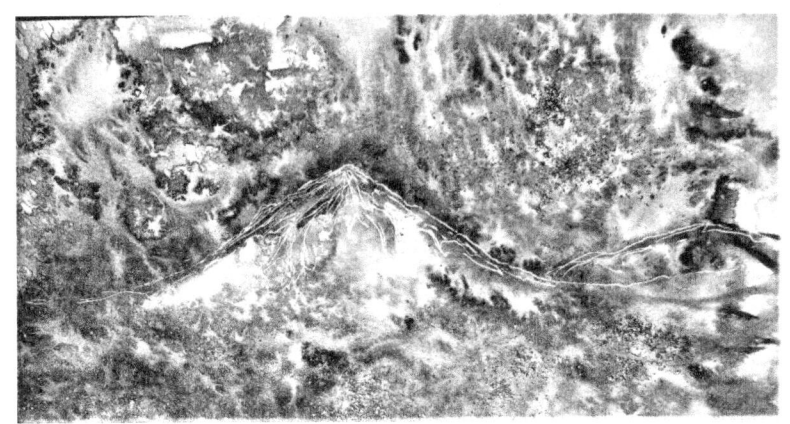
Mountain. Watercolor on paper.

Strength like a Mountain: Strong in Soft Places

The sun has no solid surface.

Most often when we think of mountains for inspiration we imagine their majesty and grandeur, high vistas, things conquered or mighty challenges to overcome. We hear stories and view photos and films about the heights, the quests, the peaks achieved, the tragedies overcome, the wildness and hardship endured! The glory! And these images are indeed empowering and sobering. Yet these do not embody the particular form of strength I want to illumine when using *Mountain* as a metaphor for trauma and healing work. Rather, I look up to the mountain as a symbol of softness; the spirit of *allowing* and the vulnerability necessary for life to grow between the hard things. Mountains rise for both kinds of inspiration.

I grew up in the Pacific Northwest, in and around Portland, Oregon. With limited other experience my sense of *Mountain* was ALWAYS about rich green and fervent growth. When you hike in the Northwest you cannot escape the lushness, the ground smothered in ferns, abundant flowers, berries, beds and shelves and hanging moss, moisture, wildlife, water. Under the watchful eye of Mt. Hood, the sensual almost ambrosial forests make up the primary experience of *Mountain.*

In my early thirties, I moved to Colorado Springs, CO. The wild and forests of Pikes Peak are completely different. You can stand in the midst of trees and see for miles. There is little or no undergrowth between the soaring brown trunks. You can walk for miles and the only green is twenty feet up where first branches protrude. It is high and dry with very little moss, far fewer babbling brooks or creeks and rivers, and by comparison, there are NO berries. More brown than green, this landscape offers its own unique kind of beauty and for a period of time in my life that difference fed me. It was what I needed; life being different, open, solitary. In my earlier undergraduate years, I had spent some time living and volunteering at a Franciscan contemplative retreat house outside of Spokane, WA. Pikes Peak wilderness brought me back to that inner silence and rest, the "waiting for clarity that would surely come."

However, I realized after a while (several years) that I had begun comparing the two and at times truly missed the lush green of home. I could lament and complain about the lack of water, lack of undergrowth and moss, the lost feeling of being held in a circle of green. Yet this was why I had purposefully come to the dry mountains, to the places of vistas and mile-high-mile-wide views, for a different kind of quiet. So, I waited. And slowly but surely, I did indeed begin to notice something new to me. I started to see what WAS growing – straight out of rock.

I found myself obsessing over the whole concept. I took photos. I drew little scenes. I wrote bad poetry about the whole emerging awareness. I focused intently on the courage and creativity and strength of the little roots of wildflowers, wild strawberries (I did find some berries) and scraggly conifers shoving themselves up and through and out of granite boulders! What a fantastic statement on what we are all capable of, breaking through stone and walls and barriers, to live! I reveled and started carefully walking around the flowering weeds breaking through cement sidewalks in the city.

And, I was missing the point (for me then) until a very different day. It was in June the day that I lay happily warming myself on a large flat boulder. Yes, the sun was shining down on me but most of the warmth I felt was coming FROM the boulder. I turned my head to ponder the flatness and warmth there and noticed on one side a little patch of wild strawberry and some sweet flowery thing sitting on top of dust, on top of rock. It was the dust which caught me. I moved closer, trying to soak in this new thing, feeling awkward like I was missing something and didn't know what, trying to let it in, when I finally saw it. There, between the crags, the big rocks and little ones, on top of this grand boulder, was a bit of dirt – a tiny spot of soil and pebbles right at the root point where the plants disappeared into rock. The roots had somehow brought up some earth with them, all the way through the boulder. Not only that, but probably some bits of boulder had broken down and become part of that soil . . . and JUST so the plants could flower and fruit and shine awhile in the sun. And they did. They shone right there, in the soft stuff of dust. That SOFT stuff I had grown up taking for granted without understanding, was also right there in between all the hard stuff. This whole mountain was NOT primarily hard after all, but only seemed that way because of how it was made – through massive upheaval of big things. But it was in the soft places *between* the big hard things, that life was still allowed to grow through, and shine.

"Asking, 'what is the meaning of life?' is the wrong question. It makes you look in the wrong places. The real question is, 'where is the meaning of life?'" (Carl Safina)

Mountains are born of struggle and challenge. Their very birth is a tale of brokenness, upheaval and violence. Whole ranges are the result of chaos: tectonic plates from the earth's crust slide and grind and bump each other, or push head to head until something pops, or otherwise erupts with enough force to cause splits and chards and whole plates and land masses to rise and crush and crunch and rise again or fall again. Sea floors suddenly become canyon walls. What once thrived underwater becomes a dry fossil on a high mountain mesa. Everything seems out of place.

In a few moments of time, what was once familiar, perhaps even peaceful and comfortable, is annihilated – and the result changes the horizon forever. Forever. Now there is a mountain born of injury, its face full of hard and broken things.

And there, too, is the soft stuff.

Between the huge hard things, is space – and in that space something else happens. Small things fill it up: broken down stones and bits of trees, sand, decaying life forms, bits of boulder, shards, twigs, fewmets, bugs, and water from the skies and new streams, all coalesce over time, transforming and becoming soil or that which can bear life.

In this vulnerable soft stuff, new life is able to seed and grow. For a fact, vast forests are born out of the SOFTNESS of *Mountain.* All the abundant life in our woods and valleys, along rivers and lake sides, is given a home because the mountain has space for things to grow. Life is allowed and continues after all the rest. In the softness, because of the broken, life finds a way.

"The clearest way to the universe is through a forest wilderness." (John Muir)

When I first lived below the eye of Pikes Peak I saw only grandeur, the bigness. I thought of the mountain as hard, solid, majestic – and distant. Then one day I took the slow train to the top and got close, standing on the top looking down, being ON that majesty. It was rubble. And I was blown away. I was blown away by the seeming sand and tiny rocks and then small rocks and slightly bigger ones all just piled up and falling apart. It didn't seem solid like I thought that meant. It was in pieces. And I was almost disappointed, until I let myself be mystified. I stood literally jaw-dropped, allowing some divine mystery to enter in, the curiosity and the NOW of it. What was it teaching me? This rubble of majesty?

"The lesson that life constantly enforces is 'look underfoot!' You are always nearer to the source of your power than you think. The lure of the distant and the difficult is deceptive. The great opportunity is where you are. Every place is the center of the world." (John Burroughs)

The difficult work of healing lays within a world of hard things, chaos, upheaval. The unforgiving injury (trauma and healing) where nothing is ever truly the same again - ever - is embodied in the same process of transformation taught to us by *Mountain*. Hard things happen. Suffering is a real part of life – no matter who you are. (Have you ever watched the news?) And there are soft spots, places between where we can allow the seeding and building up of fertile soil, the necessary waters, the growth of new life. Recognizing and naming the brokenness is one part of the process – and ONLY one part. It is helpful to experience the peaks, the courage and fortitude of climbing and overcoming, the ability to do more than you thought you could, in the face of sheer wildness to proclaim some victory, some pinnacle, a grand view of what one has overcome and come through. Again, this is only ONE part of the process.

Because then, often, another depth of healing is called upon in order to find what *else* is new, in order to experience more fully the deep transformation first set in process by upheaval and chaos, to find where new things grow from deep underneath and become abundance. This is vulnerability. This is softness needed and already present; where it is possible to be still, to let things fall apart, to let things soak in, to let things transform and affect us deeply – to let things go – and to watch things grow.

"Vulnerability sounds like the truth and feels like courage. Truth and courage are not always comfortable, but they are never weakness." (Brene Brown)

Vulnerability can be sort of a four-letter-word for many. Yet it is a necessary part of transformational healing. It is a way of allowing – and without allowing, not much grows. We learn to allow our truth to be true – no matter what that truth happens to be. We choose to stop not-wanting-to-think-about-it. We choose to take our truth out of the periphery, off the shelf, out of the closet, out from underground. Rather than clinging to the hard rock wall and feeling unseen, unknown, unheard, unmoving, like-it-is-too-hard, stuck, we learn to soften and allow.

Sometimes we are sort of forced into it. Sometimes it seems like we fall off the cliff and end up submerged in an ocean with few skills to handle it. I consider my once near-complete breakdown many years ago, one of those moments. And it was horrendous. It was also necessary. I could no longer hold on and keep going the way I was. Something had to change – give, and it was me. It was not wrong. It was just difficult. And that difficulty felt like hardness, until I learned to allow my softness – my deep and honest vulnerability – and eventually my growth. At other times a gentle nudge will let us see a new path just to the side of where we were standing before. Either way, it takes a little softness to let go.

Spending time with our vulnerable self, and all parts of Self, is about being the hero in our own story. It means going deeply into every sensation we have, every way of knowing and receiving; skills our body and spirit teach us how to do – because they know how. When we can purposefully sit with our softness we end up FEELING our story; not just the images in memory, not just the things/facts that happened or things we have overcome, or the lists of work still ahead. We give ourselves over to the feelings, feelings then and now, the ones we could not feel when all we could do was survive, the emotion still locked in our skin, muscles and bones, all our organs and our limited breathing and limited moving, limited choice.

These are the boulders we carry – the hard, broken things: the most helpless aspects of our entire journey, the times when we needed and again need help, the moments of realizing just how powerless we were and are sometimes. We carry in our bodies and spirits these burdens: the precious seconds when we stopped breathing, stopped seeing, stopped needing, stopped being present. Maybe we stopped feeling, turned rigid, (felt like granite) in order to endure. Allowing vulnerability finally, lets us finally grieve.

"If you're really listening, if you're awake to the poignant beauty and suffering of the world, your heart breaks regularly. In fact, your heart is made to break; it's purpose is to burst open again and again so that it can hold ever more wonders." (Andrew Harvey)

The strength we have within is soft like mountains are soft. It lets us cry. So very many people are afraid of their tears, or ashamed, or simply can't find them, don't believe in them, stop them, hate them – and/or had them stopped. Too many have not been allowed to feel their FULL feelings and cry all they need. And all that pent up and unrecognized, un-honored hurt stays stuck inside and makes our muscles groan, makes us ill. But the tears are like springs burst forth from deep underground, or rains that fall fresh and life-giving, providing, mixing with the muck and creating fertile ground. Tears rise up through the soft places, between the hard ones. They are soft, and yet, like tiny springs and big rivers and giant oceans, all water is the strongest force on earth, capable of breaking through and breaking down, chiseling out grand canyons and small. Life is born here. Life needs us to be softly strong.

"Nothing in the world is more gentle than water yet nothing is stronger. Water nurtures life yet cuts through solid rock. Overcome obstacles with the strength of gentleness." (the Tao #78)

As we exist and heal like a mountain we hold hard things and soft in one vast landscape of soul and self. We are never only one or only the other. We are never only the hurt and we are never apart from suffering either. If we can allow the majesty, we can allow the softness. If we can allow the heights, we can allow the depths. You cannot believe in one without the other.

"We say beneath the earth is a flowing rock. We say the flowing rock rises to the surface. We say the rock on the surface sinks toward the core of the earth, becoming molten again in turn. And we say there are breaks in the surface of the earth, places where the depths are uncovered, and it is in the broken places that the rock is transformed, and the surface of the earth is made. Where change takes places, we say, where the earth is replenished . . . ."(Susan Griffin in <u>Woman and Nature,</u> p 197 on 'our ancient rages')

When I look to MOUNTAIN now I see depth. Instead of a flat distant thing I remember viscerally the solid softness. All of our healing can be embedded and embodied in the mountains we see up high every day, and the ground which has been moved beneath our feet, wherever we are. We can embrace the beauty of the broken and vulnerable, there and here, because all of it is real, life-changing and life-giving. MOUNTAIN, both grand and humble, is a beautiful mirror. Lift up your eyes to the mountains, from whence comes your help.

Affirmations:

I am mountain. I am strong like mountains are strong. I am strong in soft places.

My vulnerability is a teacher and helper. I learn and grow through this strength.

In my broken being, I am mended with natural wholeness. I belong to the whole earth.

In my wholeness, hard places and soft, I allow life to flourish and create.

Possible questions to ask:

If my trauma experience and my healing experience are so much the same as mountains in all their process, what does that mean? Could I observe and feel the different phases in my own body?

Do I think of myself as *only* broken, and stop there? Do I lose sight of what holds me together when everything seems hard? Do I purposefully honor the life within me, the ability to heal, the healing I have done, the life I have created, the beauty that shines through me? Do I know how strong I really am? Do I stop my tears, or think they are a sign of weakness? Can I let them flow and understand the power of gentleness, or let them surge and gently change me?

Ideas for more on these themes:

-Google the authentic history and culture of Kintsugi. Consider the fact (and irony?) that gold is the softest mineral. Look into the spiritual literature on the broken vessel and the myth of the Wounded Healer.

-Research mountains in numerous spiritual traditions. Google for photos of places like Mauna Kae and Tibetan holy mountains.

-Hike your nearest mountain, especially if it is one you can look up to on a regular basis. Feel it. Get in touch with the hardness, the brokenness, the softness and the abundant life there. Look to it on a regular basis and give your time of looking at least three large, long breaths of remembrance.

-Try some plein air painting of a mountain-scape. Do it with a group. Let the image and the meaning seep into your dreams.

-stretch into the mountain yoga pose (Tadasana).

-Research how the human body is much like a mountain. What lies between the seeming hard muscle and bone?

-google Brene Brown and all her research, writing and presentations about vulnerability.

-read Andrew Harvey.

Creative non-violence connection:

The fact that vulnerability is strength, brokenness allows growth, "the crack is where the light gets in" and the softest things in creation are also the most powerful (water, gold, spirit….) flies in the face of those who misuse power through force and lies and then believe they are stronger and right. Nature teaches us this.

SELF COMPASSION. Oil on canvas.

Pearl: Transformative Power

The sun is made up of distinct layers, but without distinct borders

(like rainbows).

Most people know what a pearl looks like but may not be aware of exactly what it takes for each and every pearl to be formed.

The first ingredient is invasion.

Natural pearls are formed within the shell of a certain variety of bi-valve mollusk, from different families of saltwater clams and oysters. These animals are a keystone species: necessary to the healthy life of their surrounding environment. They have three-chambered hearts, two kidneys, digestive organs, gonads. They take a year or more to mature, growing into the shell they create themselves. They have different sexes but usually mature ambi-sexual (going back and forth over the years), or hermaphrodite (both sexes at once and able to fertilize their own eggs). In short, they are pretty amazing. The mantle is the part that produces nacre – the material used to grow its shell and form pearls as necessary. This is where "invasion" comes into the picture.

Sometimes a piece of sand, a pollutant of some kind (tiny bits of plastic) or other bit of foreign stuff, comes inside the shell while the animal is doing what it naturally does, taking water in for food and oxygen, digesting, and releasing. Usually the oyster or clam is able to dispel the foreign object. But sometimes what does not belong essentially gets stuck, lodged inside of or on the edge of the soft inner body, causing irritation: invasion.

In trauma language, the mollusk has been violated. Something which is not natural to the being has gotten inside and lodged itself as a constant irritant, threatening the well-being of the whole, even its life: shame? despair? uncontrollable rage? addiction?

In healing language, however, we can use words which focus on what is *right* rather than what is wrong. In doing so we find other themes: inner wisdom; creativity; agency and more.

"It is not necessary to wait for the gift of wholeness before beginning the work that leads to it, for when the ego sincerely

involves itself in its own redemption, the Self comes to meet and wrestle with it." (Janet O'Dallet)

When we are invaded (when suffering happens and we don't yet know how to handle it) and then come to REALIZE this (which can take years to embrace as true), we also eventually come to realize that something has to be done. Something has to change. Somehow, we need to DO something so that what is eating at us from the inside does not control or destroy us (any more). We are capable of making a decision to re-establish our larger truth, our natural way of being, free of invasion.

The mollusk is a teacher for this. Once the animal recognizes the invasion (the thing lodged and irritating its soft body) it has this miraculous, innate ability to solve the issue. This is very much a self-protective event in terms of science alone. Looking at it metaphorically and through the lens of healing, it is an act of self-compassion, inner wisdom, agency and creativity.

In true healing work three things become clear: that invasive act or event that happened or person who hurt me is still lodged inside somehow, eating away at me, limiting my fullness; there is another truth, my original innocence, and I want to know that again; there is something I can do, some capability I naturally have within, to transform it all.

Layer by layer (for the mollusk this is generally 7 to 15 years of inner work) there is this ability to pull from inside not only what is necessary to transform but the ability to use that self-made "stuff" to create something not only strong, but *intensely* strong: enough to last forever (like nano-scale brick and mortar). We call this beautiful thing a pearl.

The pearl is considered a gem, the only naturally occurring gem. It is formed by layers and layers of intricate crystalline forms aligned just perfectly with one another (slightly off rather than directly on top of each other) so that light passing along the axis of one crystal is reflected and refracted by another to produce a wave of shimmering light and color. We who look on experience the rainbow effect as it is sourced in the center and flows outward toward us. This is important: the rainbow effect is not coming from OUTSIDE the pearl. The luminescence is caused from within, from the literal structure of the pearl's being and creation.

"In the heart of a mussel shell lies the pearl of light." (Polynesian chant. Huna)

Healing growth can also be measured in terms of layers of light: pearlescent healing.

The pain we have felt from some loss or hurt, when not repaired, lodges in our soft body as memory and then we call it trauma. When the trauma causes enough irritation in our lives, it also causes us to trust some inner wisdom and bring about transformation. We move into creative action. Our self-compassion recognizes difficult things embedded unfairly and moves to create what we need. Something new and beautiful – and intensely strong - is made. The invasive thing is transformed and our new way of being restores our memory of original innocence. It was never our own fault that we were invaded. We have it within us to create our answers and experience transformation, layer by luminous layer. And when we do? Those who know us, our supporters and allies, those who love us through it all, they marvel at the inner strength and beauty that shines and is iridescent and maybe a bit mysterious.

The oyster is a teacher about innate wisdom and creative action, taking our time, self-trust and self-compassion. This is deep transformation, which is subtly (and importantly) different than simply "letting go."

Survivors of trauma are often told to let go of the past, let go of all the feelings and troubles involved. These words can sometimes border on "just get over it already," intentionally or not. Impatience, misunderstanding, denial and judgement weight this kind of advice down.

Remember, the pearl created by the mollusk lives INSIDE the shell, also of its own making, and made of the same inner material (nacre). The pearl is not let go. It remains, but it is utterly and completely transfigured. The transformative experience is not "forgotten" and neither is the original trauma. HOW that original trauma is experienced is what changes.

We cannot forget the truth of our experience, any of it, no matter what it is. We can, however, release the energies which are attached to the invasive event, our memories. We transform how the memory and the energy affects us. We continue to grow, less and less controlled or directed by the trauma. We can use all kinds of somatic methods to release what is lodged in the soft body, what has hurt for too long, what has been a seemingly mild irritant for years. But that is not the same as forgetting. Forgetting, by itself, what violence has been part of our history – individually and for whole societies and cultures – is inauthentic and leaves room for more of the same. Past hurts can provide valuable lessons and guideposts only if we allow them to be real first.

The notion that we can (and should) learn from history in order to not make the same regrettable decisions, is important.

"Never forget." (Elie Weisel)

As we release the old energies, new energies are aroused for growth. As we authentically "let go" the negative energy attached to the trauma, we find the inner, natural ability to create. Our eyes are opened to new ways of seeing the pain, new ways of seeing ourselves inside and out, new ways of seeing the world around us. Our true histories do not go away. They happened. But as the small mussel teaches us, complete transformation is also possible. We are capable of fooling ourselves or being fooled into believing this is not true. That is a lie. We can lie to ourselves. But real transformation is indeed possible because inner wisdom is stronger than the fooled mind. It is a natural reality. It happens in all of creation. Growth is not always about something brand new, but it is always about seeing things newly. Like the mussel, we are simply created this way.

"See with new eyes now

That broken piece of willow

Became your sweat lodge "

Edward Sky-Eagle, Peublo Elder.

Early in my recovery, during a time of overwhelm in terms of personal memories and emotion, I started seeing a therapist and life seemed to only get worse. I was an adult with three children. I had accomplished some things but was stuck in the turmoil. I checked myself in to a hospital because I was worried about self-harm and just going crazy. The first night I had a transformative dream.

I was a child swimming in the ocean, breathing underwater, near the top but far enough below the waves that it was calm. I could see the turbulence above me, where waves crashed back and forth. I could feel the calm around me, the warmth and pressure against my skin. I looked around at the various life forms swimming by without minding me. I looked up and looked down. It was like a moment of decision as to which way to swim. Down to the ocean floor was a very long way and I was not sure I could breathe underwater forever, or handle the pressure, or the immense silent calm, or what might lurk down there. But the light allowed me some direction and I could see the plant life at the bottom and I felt impelled to start slowly swimming down. On the ocean floor I could stand and much of the pressure was gone. I saw a small grouping of plants and a small shell sitting there. It had barnacles all over it, and was mostly dark in color, seaweed stuck to it, mostly closed. I picked it up and opened it. There was a pearl. It felt like a gift. I woke up.

This dream has guided me for a long time. It is about the promise of finding the answers within, and inner wisdom hard-won. It is invasion turned new. It is trauma and healing. It is the wounded healing and wounded healer. It is using one's own story, your truth as hard as it might be, becoming your own hero, as difficult as that might be, and creating something lovely, something maybe even loving, giving of its luminosity.

"The holiest of spots on earth are where the ancient hatred has become a present love." (A course in Miracles)

It isn't easy, this path. But it is worth it.

Natural pearl formation is actually rare. Most mollusks are able to excrete enough mucus to simply spit irritants out. Most children have enough support and are given the tools and skills to deal with whatever comes their way in life. Most people do not experience overwhelming suffering, but some do. Most children do not have caregivers purposefully hurting them because of their own sickness, but some do. Would that we did not have to see war and famine and injustice everywhere in the world on the daily news. That is the truth. But there are answers and the attached pain can be transformed. When we choose a healing path we find the gems– pearls of great price.

Sometimes people say that healing is hard as hell. Me? I think of it as hard as heaven. It can be *easy* to stay stuck in self-defeating patterns. True transformation is hard.

The work is worth it. The luminosity is worth it. As you accept that the pain is there you make a choice: live with it as it is killing you, or not. It is a choice which requires that we go looking and find the thing stuck, and name it. It means fully accepting that there is this stuck thing and it hurts. It means getting to know this thing SO WELL that you also know what you have to do, well. As you begin the layered work of healing you get stronger and stronger along the way. There comes a time when you no longer identify with the fact of the lodged pain, no longer are spell-bound with limiting beliefs and conditions. With each new layer of healing work, life changes and our eyes are opened further. Eventually we no longer see that old thing: it has no more power. What we see instead is the crystalline architecture of beauty and luminescence, shining with strength. Our focused consciousness, sourced from within, makes us agents of change in our own lives. Individually and collectively, we are the heroes in our own novel, our own best medicine on all levels. It is like spiritual homeopathy: what we need for healing is already inside of us. We know how to do it.

We are also, as we do the work, sources of life and beauty for others, medicine for the planet. We can find the ways needed to take care of all the orphaned children everywhere, inside and out, transforming the invasive forces around them. We are, all, keystone species. Thanks be to the universe of all being for the tiny powerful oyster as a teacher.

Affirmations:

I am innocent. I embrace original innocence. I am free of the old things that held me down and back. I choose to transform those things.

I have what I need within me to re-embody my softness, to create my own shell of protection, and create beauty.

I take what comes and know that suffering is real in my life and all lives, but I take that awareness and make something new, something different, something that gives light and reflects light.

I am strong. I am beautiful. I shine. I am luminous from the inside. I am a gem. I am a pearl of light, and great price.

I share my light and I help others to find theirs.

Possible questions to ask:

If my trauma experience and my healing are so much the same as the process of a pearl being made, what does that mean? Can I feel and observe all the different phases in my own body?

If I were suddenly on my deathbed, what would I wish I had done differently, figured out, delved into, healed? Are there things I have been avoiding for too long – old traumas, or new and current pains un-healed, still invading who I most truly am? Do I accept the fact that this harms my relationships with others, even hurts others too? Do I believe I have everything I need inside to deal well with everything and fully recover and remember my deepest true self? What can I do to help others know they are capable of transforming their pain, too?

For more on these themes:

-Google Pearl and research some of the myriad references for what the pearl stands for or symbolize, and the many different myths about how they are formed. The most interesting (to me) google link led me to the "blue pearl," a hindu concept which aligns the pearl with the third eye and pineal gland, psychic experience and the sixth, ajna, chakra, divine seeing and attunement.

-write an article about what causes you suffering, then a poem about your wisdom in dealing with that loss.

-write a letter to a perpetrator (person or institution). Tell them you are changing them, you are turning them into light and they no longer have the power to invade and cause pain.

-consider the pearl every time you see a rainbow. Let it remind you of your own creative beauty.

-if there are children in your lives, help them to repair their pains in creative ways.

Creative non-violence connection:

Forgetting what has caused suffering, denying the violence done to others and/or ourselves, or to the earth, enables violence to continue. It is only in fully naming and embracing our pain that we can fully embrace our true, gentle, power for creative action. Non-violent action depends on the power of deep attention to the other so they too can be warriors of light.

BECOMING. Watercolor and gel pen on paper.

The Unfolding Flower

All plants need sunlight in order to photosynthesize. They then store that energy in roots or tubers, continuing to process that light during what is called a dark phase, until the plant is ready to grow.

It is easy to think about blooms. It is easy to think about flowers. But there is something important that happens BETWEEN those two states in a plant; something very essentially different. The unfolding flower is not really a *thing*. It is a process. It is a creative action and something which *happens,* usually when we are not watching. We see a plant, bush, tree, before there are flowers, and we see the resulting flower after it has bloomed, but we do not really "see" the process of blooming. Yet it happens. Always. Always it is happening.

"Everything tends toward awakening" Isamu Nagachi

My daughter and I happen to love Morning Glories. This is a vining plant that grows mostly in spring and summer whose blooms open and close each day, in tune with the coming and going of light. We have spread their tiny black seeds and planted them for years because we love them. They vine all over the place, wherever, and then they flower. They grow buds which open when the sun comes up and close when the sun goes down – or as the earth turns. We have each sat and watched, tried to catch the moment when the curled, closed up flower suddenly opens and shares its glory, facing the sun. It isn't sudden though. It is slow and deliberate, and hard to "catch" with normal eyesight. Our brains don't seem to comprehend the event as it is happening. Even as we are watching, we don't "see" it, we just know that there wasn't a flower before and now there is one. It is a quiet, slow happening. Cameras can capture it, and when my daughter was very young she used to capture it in a kind of slow dance, starting all curled up on the floor and slowly standing and moving and opening. But natural blooming is beyond our ability to plan, or force, or even see. Yet it happens, in its own time.

A plant of any kind needs to have the ideal conditions externally; the right amount of water, air, earth, temperatures, cycles of light, pollination, bees. And it needs the right conditions internally; the storage of the sun's energy, the natural wisdom to pay attention and "know" when it is time to break open a seed, sprout new growth, produce a bud, flower, close a bloom, let a bloom die, shut down again, begin again. This is all seemingly slow though happening all at once, and all the change is dependent on many things coming together just right and paying attention. The Morning Glory is not just one flower but a vine full of leaves and flowers which individually come and go, open and close, die and birth from Spring into Fall.

Healing is very similar. It is not a "thing" either. It is not even "a" process. It IS process. There is no END to it, no moment in time when one can say, "Ah, today I am fully healed." The universe is still moving; storms will still come. We are connected to the rest of the planet and all its suffering people. We do not "become healed." We heal. It is an unfolding: a constant process of opening and closing, dying and birthing.

The process of unfolding is true of all life forms, animate and seemingly inanimate. And, all unfolding is connected – in the same way that each unique flower is connected to a vine. My healing is connected to your healing and is like your healing. Our healing is connected to the work of all being and is *like* the work of all beings. All of us belong to a universe that works in constant patterns of unfolding and revealing.

"When we look into the heart of a flower, we see clouds, sunshine, minerals, times, the earth, and everything else in the cosmos in it. Without clouds there could be no rain, and there would be no flower. Without time the flower could not bloom. In fact, the flower is made entirely of non-flower elements; it has no independent, individual existence. It 'inter-is' with everything else in the universe." Thich Nhat Hahn

This unfolding involves a lot of history – all of it - how we got where we are whether that has been hard or easy or the mix of those. Then it requires setting up the right conditions for growth. Then it requires patience, mindful waiting and watching. And it requires we trust ourselves and the process. We go about our work day by day and trust that it is happening. It is most easy to look backwards and see how we have grown from the past, how we are no longer the same. Sometimes it is easy to look forward to where we are going. But being present to our healing NOW requires a kind of mindfulness, awareness, presence, consciousness, deliberate actions, discipline, vigilance, patience and trust.

Like all things, plants growing or people, the changes necessary for unfolding are dependent on not just external things (health, self-care, support, inspiration....) but internal things as well. What are our sources internally that allow our natural wisdom to "know" when it is time? Time to grow, evolve, let go, force something, lay low, rest, push, hope, do-nothing, open up, close up, bloom? And how do we make ourselves aware of this inner wisdom? I don't think we have to put words on it all, or always have it carefully defined, but it is helpful to be aware, to "know thyself," and put our/your own words on it.

There are ways to remind ourselves, to be conscious of the fact that this internal/external circle is in fact going on, and internally we WILL know "when it is time" and we will grow. As the seed that knows when to open, as the vine that knows when to bud, as the bud that knows when to bloom, as the flower that knows when to die – we heal. This is evidence of a deep kind of resonance: movement within which is in tune with movement without, and vis-versa. What is going on inside is affected by and affects the external world, and vis-versa.

I believe strongly that one piece of this awareness belongs solely to the body. There are so very many somatic methods, techniques, practices, new and ancient, whose underlying intention is to help us be conscious of what is going on in our bodies – our bodies wherein the inner wisdom lives and has its being. Just like the morning glory has to listen to its body, the vine and leaves and roots, it has to wait for the right warmth and light, a "feeling" in the body of the plant, we on a healing path have to pay attention and learn the attunements of our seasons: what gives us warmth, what nourishes, what "feels" right while we transition, what do we need while we wait through a dark night? When it is time to grow, what kind of growth is the right kind? When it is time to unfold and flower – how will we know which direction and how high and how fast? It is in the body, this wisdom. And in that same incarnated wisdom is the psyche, the soul, the spirit, the Self – the truth of our being.

"The Hawaiian word for body is Kino, 'a sacred plant consisting of aimed thought.' And, the word for 'regaining consciousness' is the same as the word which means 'to open as flower petals." (Rima A Morell, PhD.)

Listening to the body, and becoming aware that wisdom is at work, invites conscious intention. The mind is involved. Sometimes intention requires courage. It asks us to take a risk, to go ahead and act upon what we think might be going on. If we are going to start as a small seed in dark earth, and end up four feet above ground, or vining for fifteen feet, and then producing bulbs and more seeds and then flowering brightly for all to see --- there are many moments of risk, intention and courage. Each one is unique and worth honoring. Life is not actually about repetition alone. Even the next fractal formed has never been before. Always, all things are made new – integrating with this, dis-integrating with that, and so on, forever. What you are thinking or picturing right now, has never been thought before in just the same way as now. This movement has never been done. This day has never happened before. Your next breath has never been breathed. Each piece of the circle of growth is important. The courage to pay attention, trust the wisdom and allow growth in its right timing, is important. And as any on the path of healing can share – the risk which lets courage emerge, is worth it.

"Nature loves courage. You make a commitment and nature will respond to that commitment by removing obstacles. Dream the important dream and the world will not grind you under, it will lift you up ...." (Terence McKenna)

Sometimes regular growth is thwarted. Sometimes plants die because the right season came too late, or too early.

Sometimes plants are walked on, yanked up for some reason, peed on, chemically altered, sprayed with poisons, run over, thunderstruck. Trauma happens. It always will. Everywhere. So, is it still possible to grow? To someday bloom?

    Flowers alone are intensely fragile. They are utterly vulnerable to the elements, and children, and people who like flowers in vases, to animals and wind, hail and so much more. But they generally find a way to flower again, to risk the unfolding. Are we this capable, no matter what? To be who we are meant to be? To intend, to live our courage, to risk unfolding, to bloom? Yes. Because, like flowers, we belong to something bigger, the bigger plant, the larger earth, the wisdom inherent everywhere in everything which proves that suffering and dying do not end life and the capacity for growth. All things transform. Energy moves and changes. It continues. And plants especially just keep proving themselves capable, through seasons and composting and volcanoes, fires, floods and kids.

    Next time you walk down an old, cracked sidewalk, be sure to give space to the small buds popping through. They are there to unfold and bloom. Like you, they are waiting for their moment.

"I sit before flowers, hoping they will train me in the art of opening up." (Shane L. Koyczan, contemporary poet)

Flowers flower, they unfold at the right time. Who else can determine the right time to risk? The right time to share? The right time to hibernate and go deep within? The right time to grieve? Or how long it takes? No one. Trust yourself.

The unfolding flowering is also a lesson in choice. It can be very important to choose where we heal and who will support us. And when it is going well? We can be grateful. We can honor those times when we find ourselves "in the heart of the world caught in the descending radiance…" (Teilhard de Chardin, <u>Hymn of the Universe</u>) These are moments when everything seems to be coalescing and happening just right. We all have these times and can treasure them.

Often as survivors of trauma we might hold back and wait for the next shoe to drop. But we don't always have to, and can learn not to. We can choose to transform that old habit. We can choose to learn how to follow the flow, allow the grace, believe in the synchronicity, and give ourselves fully to the moment, the descending radiance. Those are the times when we feel in touch with who we really are deeply and truly, whether or not our direction is clear in day to day life.

"The most important kind of freedom is to be what you really are." (Jim Morrison)

Choice is about freedom. We could in fact choose to NOT grow in certain ways, but it would feel bad. We could choose to NOT learn from inspirations and lessons along the way, NOT learn that going down that path inevitably leads to a swamp, to NOT learn that this person who bothers me so much is bringing something up in me that I actually, desperately want to understand and transform – but these choices can make us feel bad. We are free to choose to NOT be who we are built within to be. We are also free to unfold into absolutely the way we are meant to shine forth and keep going. How about we choose to pay attention to what our own bodies are telling us, what our emotions have to say, what wisdom comes in our breathing and moving?

"Deep inside the caverns of your own body there is outrageous creativity. Your feelings and emotion are carriers of wisdom, but they cannot send their gifts unless you allow them to unfold and illuminate within you.... There is no higher spirituality than the direct transmission of your own body." (Matt Licatta)

DO I SEEK LIGHT? OR DOES LIGHT SEEK ME?

This teacher, the unfolding flower, helps us to realize that it is mostly a matter of light seeking itself, this process we are in.

The light stored within recognizes the embracing light from without, and we turn to each other. THAT is a celebration!

This teacher also guides us to know that "being healed" is not necessarily the goal. The goal is to be the process, and sometimes in the process we live the beauty and fragrance of a flower. Sometimes we are the one dying and letting go seed. Sometimes we are the waiting, the paying attention, the slowness, the discerning spirit rooted in earth and reaching for sky, sometimes we are stepped on. All of it is the process. All of it can be held in our unfolding. We do not unfold TO become. The unfolding IS the becoming.

Perhaps it is time for some blooming tea. These are bags of tea leaves wrapped around a dried flower. As you sit with your warm cup, the flower unfolds in your cup. This makes me smile!

Affirmations:

I embody the energy of an unfolding flower.

My body, mind and spirit know what I need to grow.

I set my face toward the light and shine my glorious beauty.

I belong to the universe. I AM how all things move and have their being.

There is a source within and without which hold my process.

I choose the healing way which is mine, my way to bloom.

Possible questions to ask:

If my experience of trauma and healing can be described as much the same as how flowers unfold, what does that mean? Can I observe the same phases and changes in my own body?

What gets in my way when I think I am lost, on the wrong path, have strayed from my true being? Have I sought out the right people and places to be and things to do which will help me come back to my inner wisdom and ability to grow? Am I afraid to grow? Am I afraid of my own beauty? What will it feel like to bloom and shine freely in the light? Have I felt that before? Is that part of my original innocence? What changes are being asked of me? Where in my body can I tell there is a need for movement? What is going on in my external world that matches what is going on internally? Where does my nourishment come from, my watering? Do I allow myself to be beloved enough to be watered as I need it? Am I willing to risk, to make choices according to what I know? To grow, change, vine, bush, bud, bloom, die, create seeds to continue? Where is my best garden? What do I need to grow and unfold and bloom as is truly best for me? Where am I unfolding now?

For more on these themes:

- Look up and practice: the unfolding flower yoga movement – or any of the somatic therapies and practices. Learn ways to let your body be your teacher and guide.

-let yourself dance like a flower unfolding.

- next time you see a flower, and as often as possible...stop for them.... The way to gain freedom from "it's just a flower" emerges directly from how consciously we engage with it.

-check YouTube for amazing videos of flowers blooming in slow motion, as well other plants blooming in jungles and forests around the world.

-Consider following the online blog of Matt Licata PhD, psychotherapist, retreat director, author and teacher based in Boulder, CO.

Creative non-violence thought:

It is essential to grasp the dignity of all beings. A non-violent lifestyle is as much about trusting your own unfolding as about trusting the process in others. Your heart is what touches other hearts, but always and only, each blooms in their own time. Nature teaches us this.

Galway Kinnel poem of St Francis and the Sow

The bud

Stands for all things,

Even for those things that don't flower

For everything flowers from within, of self-blessing;

Though sometimes it is necessary

To re-teach a thing it's loveliness. To put a hand on its brow

Of the flower

And we tell it in words and a touch

It is lovely

Until it flowers again from within, of self-blessing

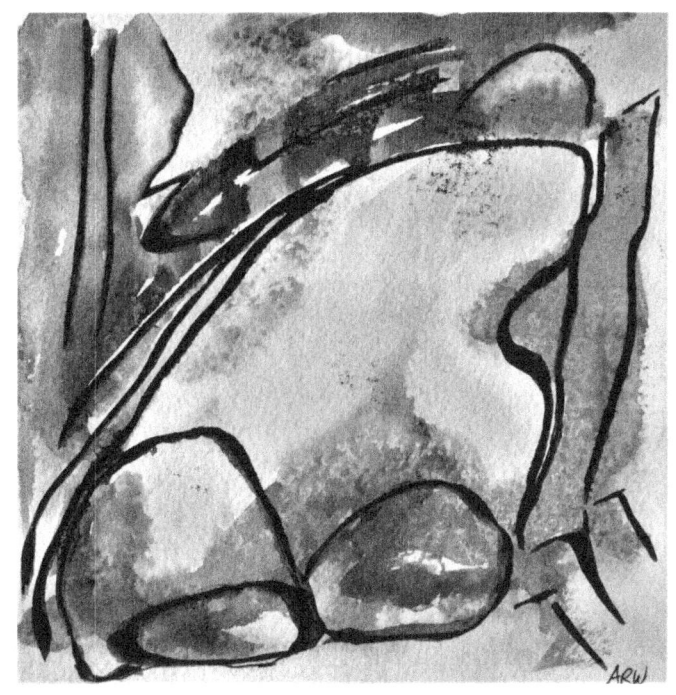

STONES. Watercolor and ink on paper.

Stones: Witness and Honoring

The sun is estimated to have been "born" 4.5 million years ago, and this is considered "young." There is enough energy being made and transformed to last at least 5 billion more years.

> "If you were to peer into the heart of a stone at the atomic level, you would not see a dead, inert mass of material, but a furiously whirling mini-cosmos." (Wu Wei)

As a young child, I collected stones. I recall my bedroom floor in 2nd grade, where all my clothes and necessities were in a pile on the floor while in the bottom of my dresser drawers and the floor of my closet, around a couple pots of water, were stones. Rocks. I loved to hold them, put them in water and then see the differences, stare.... I think I talked to them. I was that kind of kid. As I have aged I have moved numerous times and brought stones with me, cans of rocks, literally. I have made stone circles, stone altars, stone piles.... I kept stones in secret places, in pockets, on windowsills, asked people traveling to bring me stones from faraway places, sat in rivers for hours just marveling at the rocks, playing with their colors and changes in the water and air (I had people refer to me as a "cheap date" because that is all I really wanted to do, really). These days I have a favorite field where I get to lay on the ground, right in the center of a labyrinth laid out in stones. I have rocks on my windowsills and bookshelves. I am careful about moving them. My kids are tired of my rocks, and don't give me much time when I want to show them a new neat one. At 56, it is all still a thing.

But things we do in life, especially things we started doing as children, are not truly just accidents. Small and big passions have specific reasoning and purpose. Little rituals no one else knows about, have meaning. We are all, always, seeking out how to make unconscious things more conscious, or finding ways to simply live by what those things mean – to be true to them.

So why? Why stones? What qualities in stones did I need so much to have them be such a big part of my life, then and continuing? There are many aspects to stones, to simple rocks, which apply and I can't cover them all in a small chapter: things like endurance; resilience; change over time; diversity; hardness; softness; the holding of fossil forms; building up from sand; breaking down from mountain; and doing it all again; holding form and changing form; being the soft stuff within which diamonds are formed, and the hard stuff around which rivers flow; being vulnerable to the gentle force of water; being dust and more dust piling up in just the right ways; being walked on, used for building, carved into, thrown about . . .. There are so many options for living metaphors of healing. I've chosen three themes and hope they are helpful: truth-telling; honoring the milestones and giving witness; and the essence of connection.

"...Perhaps crystals and stones are especially apt symbols of the Self because of the 'just-so-ness' of their nature.... In this sense the stone symbolizes what is perhaps the simplest and deepest experience of something eternal that man can have in those moments where he feels immortal and unalterable." (Carl Jung)

Stones tell the truth. They do not lie. What they are is exactly what they are. Where they came from, how they have changed, is exactly where they came from and how they have changed. How they are still holding together is just that. They are. They stand for truth and they do it in a very right here-right now way. If you miss the glimmering beauty of a river rock today, it might not be there tomorrow. If you walk over the gravel in your driveway today, and do not notice, you may not have the same chance tomorrow. Stones are about the truth RIGHT NOW. They are opportunities, pure opportunity, to be with what is real, right now.

I think this idea that stones are about the immediate present, and that they therefore do not lie, was very important for me as a child and young person. This is still a force in the kind of person I choose to be. When there is trauma, it is so easy, and necessary at times, to be AWAY from NOW ---to escape in some way, to dissociate (psych-lingo), to see something ELSE than what is happening or what all the feelings are, to get away from confusion, to be the littler girl pretending that what was sad was happening to someone else. As unhealed adults the patterns continue or we just choose to "get away" from NOW (global traumas and our personal ones) via numerous methods. Denial, addiction, obsession, hyper-activity, depression, uncontrollable rage, sheer avoidance (like I am just not willing to see that news anymore) – all are different ways to NOT be present. And they work, until we want something else.

But rocks hold presence. When I was young they were a thing I could hold that kept me in my body while giving me something strong and beautiful and sure, something true. As a child I needed to inwardly separate from a deeply troubled family. But the stones gave me something solid and true, something ELSE real and ok in the present. Not only is there nothing wrong with that, it was actually a pretty powerful thing to do. I would put rocks in my water bin and see them change. I played with them, let them run through my fingers, saw them. There was resonance: I saw them and they saw me. I held them and they held me. We understood each other. I believe this.

"There is a proverb that a human being is stronger than a stone and more tender than a flower." (Habib Rahman, brother of Gul Rahman (prisoner #24) who died in CIS custody at Guantanamo)

That was me, present to myself, strong and tender at once. Both were true then. Both are still true, but as an adult I have more ability to realize what is happening, to observe the resonance, to feel it in my body with awareness and curiosity. I truly believe the more we can attune our traumas to what nature is doing, the more profound our healing can be. Changing the language in my head to say that my trauma and healing are so much like a mountain, a pearl being formed, an unfolding flower, a stone, etc. . . . inherently implies resilience, process, endurance, sustainability, transformation. I experience this in body and soul.

There was another thing I would do with my boxes and buckets of rocks. Sometimes many, or just one at a time, I would take them out and put them somewhere new – the creek, a field, a pile I built up in a secret place. They were like little monuments declaring that I was there, and that something happened. The small cairns gave witness.

Apparently, humans have always – like forever from day one – used rocks to create monuments, to honor things, to be a place of memorial and inspiration and remembrance. We have used stones to say, "HEY! Something important happened!!!!" We have said it to each other, and we have also been happy to say it to the stars, the universe, the cows in the field, the birds who stop by, the bugs who crawl around our piles of stones ritually built and left as a statement: something has happened. "I was here."

In our healing work, it can be really helpful, and really important, to honor and remember our "happenings" along the way. At hard times it is helpful to be able to look back and say… "Oh, remember when I didn't know this?" "I remember when I finally realized that." "Look at how far I have actually come"….. Sometimes healing does not feel like accomplishment. It just feels hard. So we put up hard monuments in honor of hard, hard things.

Sometimes we create altars or stone sculptures to honor some milestone or achievement. Honoring our growth spots can be pretty important – hard ones and easier ones. Things we've overcome and things we've just barely gotten through. We're all on a journey and there are things to remember and honor along the way. Stones are good witnesses. If you are reading this, and it means anything at all, then you have come somewhere. You've been on a journey and there are milestones along the way.

Maybe some of those things are moments we would like to forget about: maybe things we think back on as mistakes. I sometimes take a stone and carry it around for a while in my pocket or bag. I let something I'm working on - a challenge, a "mistake," a trouble with another person, a social issue which hurts, something that needs change and transformation - become that stone. I carry it until something new happens and then I do something new with the stone. I put it in a cairn, place it in a new place, or I throw it in a river or some body of water to symbolize that I have come to see that the entire situation is bigger than me and I let it go, or to enact my anger with bodily release. Things like this are about remembering, changing and honoring. Sometimes we remember the pain and release it. Sometimes we remember the courage or the new-found peace and honor that. Sometimes it is for our selves and sometimes it is for others, or for all of us as we are all connected.

"Hear stand the mean, uncomely stone, tis cheap in price! The more it is despised by fools, the more loved by the wise." (Verse by the alchemist Arnaldus de Villanova referring to the alchemist stone, the lapis both despised and rejected.)

Veteran's walls, Fireman's walls, victims of 9-11 wall of names, the great wall of prayer. These are not the most beautiful or uplifting monuments in terms of the feelings brought about, and yet they are vital statements of witness, and we cannot leave these places alone – also because of the feelings brought about. The stone monuments help us to say, "I was here. This happened" as well as "You were here. We will not forget." "SEE ME!" "I SEE YOU." We remember, and it is good for us to do so.

Stones give witness. Witness is not only a solitary act. To witness and honor growth and change and that "something happened" is a shared thing. We *see* each other's monuments and markings and honorings and memorials. This aspect of witness is about empathy. Being survivors of trauma brings with it a responsibility to also know and bear witness to and honor the memorials of others who know suffering. Suffering and change are shared truths. It is only right to honor that fact in others as well as ourselves. We are stones for each other. Compassion is something to hold and let grow and share.

"I will speak to you in stone-language (Answer with a green syllable)

I will speak to you in snow-language (Answer with a fan of bees)

I will speak to you in water language (Answer with a canoe of lightening)

I will speak to you in blood-language (Answer with a tower of birds)." (Octavio Paz)

There have also been times in my life of rock-loving when the stones were too large, or too stuck in the ground to take home or move. Then I had a place to sit, or lie, or a boulder to hug or sit under, to come back to. At those times especially, I had a sense of being heard, felt, known and held. My whole body got to feel the whirling-cosmos within. Limbic resonance. Mirroring. All those research and trauma words, also metaphors, were lived. These are scientific metaphors for connection.

The "limbic resonance" with stones is maybe like sound - which may "sound" weird but give it a chance. Often while laying on a boulder, or holding one with a deep sense of silence, the "feeling" level has always been similar to that gorgeous sense of connection one might feel while crying through a symphony or opera, some favorite piece of music you feel deeply – you resonate with. There is something about sound.

"Crystals are living beings at the beginning of creation. All things have a frequency and a vibration." (Nikola Tesla)

Maybe sound is connection, even if all we do is hum, or move, or pray, or breathe.

"The word 'prana' coming from the root 'AN,' to breathe, signifies not only human breath but the breath of the Universe, the life force. It is thus similar to 'chi' in Taoism, 'ruach' in Judaism, and 'pneuma' in Greek thought. It is the tendency of the unmanifest to vibrate and take form." (From the Kaushitaki Upanishad)

There is current research being done where folks are saying that the stones of Stonehenge actually give off a kind of sound . . . a vibration which can be felt, if not heard by the eardrums and brain. Music – perhaps all things are made of music. That kind of connection, through stones, is deep connection. Stones help us know that throughout change, we belong. Perhaps we already know how stones capture energy, like sound. This is why we honor our loved ones with stones.

Stones actually live out the sense of continuity that our entire universe is always trying to sing to us. "I am here – despite the chaos, in lieu of the changes, in and through the changes. We are here, together." With stones I have felt the aura of companionship, sometimes palpably. And these experiences have often brought me to song, or a chant, or just an audible "ooh."

I literally have a few rocks in particular, favorites, I have had for years and years. I remember exactly where I found them, and I will in fact sometimes hum to them, just hold them and hum, or do meditation, deep breathing. I know they hear me and help me. Call me crazy and I will bring you a stone to sing with.

The Hawaiians have a saying, "your stone will find you."

A final point about stones also works well as a metaphor for healing. They are all about change. Sand breaks down to silt travels in water and air to new places becomes something hard and new again becomes small boulders and big mountain remains broken becomes sand and goes where the river runs through it. The essence is real, within the changes, at once new and the same because it is now part of the larger essence, the all of it all stuff.

From out of my old Roman Catholic theology (which I have grown away from) this is an aspect of healing I link up with the word, "transubstantiation." This is about real presence and deep internal change, while still remaining as I am and have always been outwardly. It is still my body and my blood: the suffering happened. The history is real. But my inner essence of being, is transformed so completely that now when I look at the simple facts of the matter…. I see with new eyes. I am made new and my true and deepest essence is held newly.

So, even while all things are about flux, stones are also "solid" in their truth. They do not lie. In one way or another they hold our story and "speak" it. Others know, something, when they see your cairns and memorials. Honor your journey with stones and let them hum your presence forever.

"According to Huna, when you make a journey, you chant to the place you are traveling to, or in a deep sense, creating, for no one else will have your experience there. Every meeting is a blend of your consciousness with the power of that particular place." (Rima A, Morrell PhD.)

Affirmations:

I am solid. I change.

I endure. I transform.

I resonate with the inner heart of stones and other natural elements like trees and rivers.

My healing journey does have milestones along the way because I have already come far.

I am free to honor every single milestone alone the way.

I honor the pain, the grief, the journey, the overcoming and the joy of others who have struggled, their journey and sorrow and endurance, their loss and their courage.

Possible questions to ask:

If aspects of my experience of trauma and healing are like stones, and how stones change and endure, what does that mean? Can I observe this in my body, feel the hum maybe?

Can I name the milestones in my journey? Are there things in my life I have forgotten to honor in a tangible way? Are there things in my life which already feel like boulders too hard to carry, that maybe I could just be with, or make them small in my pocket for a while instead? Do I sometimes deny how far I have come or how well I am doing? When I am inspired by others on the healing path, how do I honor them? Do I do the same for myself?

ideas for more on these themes:

- Create a circle of stones within which you can sit or stand or lay inside, where each rock represents an important person in your life. Spend time resonating with your whole story.
- Create a line of stones in a field, or a small cairn, build a little building with stones – in a field, in your yard, in an alley – where each stone is a milestone. Let it be in a place you can come back to and remember.

- Carry a stone in your pocket or bag for a time, weeks, months. Let it represent a person, a meaningful place, a strength, a challenge, something to let go of, a goal. You will know when it is time to give that stone a new home.
- Google the images of ancient cairns. Visit them.
- Visit a graveyard and touch the stones that have been carved in honor of strangers.
- Choose a stone to honor your journey and place it by your doorway. Touch it when you pass in and out your door. Remember how far you have come.

NON-VIOLENCE connection:

I believe everyone interested in nonviolence today could learn a great deal from the actions and ways of the people of Standing Rock. Research the 2016-17 nonviolent stance against DAPL in North Dakota. Much of their work was done while visibly and audibly praying, chanting and drumming for the good of all people, including those trying to stop them.

DESCENDING INTO LIGHT. Reverse photo of clay sculpture.

Compost: Descending Into Light

Approximately 1 trillion neutrinos from the sun will pass through your body while you read this sentence.

Compost: noun, verb

1. A mixture of organic matter, as from leaves and manure, that has decayed naturally or been digested by various organisms, used to provide nutrients and otherwise improve the structures and abilities of soil.
2. The process of transforming or converting organic matter.
3. To fertilize with reconstituted organic matter.

If you have ever been a gardener, or if you have walked in a moist wood in the Fall or early Spring, then you have experience with this teacher. The smells alone are a memory worth re-kindling, and every exuberant moment of flowering and seasonal harvesting could be one great "thank you" to this process of dying, death and transformation.

For the person willing to know the truth and reality of trauma in their life (big and small), these transformations in our backyards are meaningful and inspirational. In fact, it is possible to look upon this process of breakdown with awe and gratitude. We can learn to hold a certain appreciation for what De Chardin named so well:

"... an overwhelming sympathy for all that stirs within the dark mass of matter." (Teilhard De Chardin in <u>Hymn of the Universe</u>)

By *now* as you have read this page, maybe five or six trillion more tiny subatomic particles have passed through you. The science may be complex but one of the ways these tiny masses are produced is in what is called radioactive decay – such as occurs in the nuclear reactions of the sun. About 65 billion solar neutrinos pass from the sun through the earth, one square centimeter at a time, every second. Like just now. And now again. Again. The magnitude of this event, and the smallness, both contribute to the mystery, and our awe. All these little electromagnetic somethings simply pass unimpeded through all of earth's mass – including our bodies.

It is very much like what we can see when we notice light traveling through transparent material, such as a window. And like what we feel then, though scientifically it is not the same thing, it is very much LIKE an experience of warming. The sun's energy is constantly and deeply penetrating us all, LIKE warmth, and thus causing change. In the center of your compost pile it is warm, even too hot to touch, because of all the little reactions and transformation going on. In your backyard, in the field next door, in the moist forest floor, this process is going on inches, feet and multiple layers below the surface.

I love knowing that what we experience as "the dead of winter," when what we see with our eyes is barren and cold, death-like and unmoving, the earth itself is at its most vibrant and active phase of being. What is below the surface is MORE ALIVE than ever with movement and change, recycling, transformation, dying and birthing. Hence, the power of compost.

Healing from trauma is so often like this. There is a core, a place below the surface of our daily lives, the HEART of the matter, the heart of our being, the heart of our continuing, which is hot with possibility. It is fecund. Perhaps what we are aware of feeling is above ground, more like winter. Perhaps we feel despair, depression, a deep sadness, a dying. Perhaps we are overwhelmed by the trauma around us, or our own or both. We are winter-like, feeling barren and cold. There are times like that, whole seasons. And all the while, this mass of fecund material is alive and churning, deep within. It is there awaiting the right moment, the right signs, the right awareness, the right path, the right time.

"Shall I not have intelligence with the earth? Am I not partly leaves and vegetable mould myself? "(Walt Whitman in <u>Song of Myself</u>)

Composting demands that the leaf and vegetable mold break down, fall apart, become a pile of pieces. Along the healing path, breaking down is not easy to do, but is sometimes necessary and often best. One of my favorite authors describes the psychological process of break-down in just such ways. She describes it as *"a creative process which, like the paradoxical genius of nature itself, aims towards wholeness, a moonlike condition in which light and dark are of equal value and import."* (*Janet O Dallet in* <u>When the Spirits Come Back.</u>)

"*There is in all things an invisible fecundity, a dimmed light, a meek namelessness, a hidden wholeness."* (Thomas Merton)

This hidden wholeness is in our core and is the system by which we are each made up. The path that leads to integration and discovering our hidden wholeness is very much like Autumn, the time of breakdown and death-like changes. Yet deep inside the **light** is warming, and still passing through unimpeded. After the break down, healing happens.

After the breakdown, and *because* of the breakdown, healing happens.

"There is a dark place within/ where hidden and growing our true spirit rises, beautiful/ and tough as chestnut/ stanchions against (your nightmare of weakness) / ...and of impotence. These places of possibility within ourselves are dark because they are ancient and hidden; they have survived and grown strong through that darkness...." (Audre Lourde)

Surviving and growing strong: these are the gifts of doing the difficult enduring work. Indeed, when we do it well and consciously, when we embrace the dying and the necessary changes which come with grieving what we have lost, what we never had, and what has happened . . . then grief becomes a path of awakening. Like compost, the process of breaking down and being re-warmed in the darkness, allows for the inner light to give life again. Deep in the heart of the compost blackness there is still the workings of the sun. Deep in our darkest night there is still the workings of our spirit. In that heat, which can burn like fire, the sun has given its gift and life continues. The darkness does not overcome it.

"... Now I am terrified at earth! It is that calm and patient... It grows such sweet things and out of such corruptions ... Great is life... and real and mystical... wherever and whoever, Great is death. Sure as life holds all parts together, sure as the stars return again after they merge into light, death is great as life...." (Walt Whitman in <u>Leaves of Grass</u>)

Still, most of us fear this process and avoid it at all cost. We take it only in tiny bits and pieces. We deny that it is happening or that it needs to happen. We try to be FINE. But this life-shattering work, this breaking down of what we held onto before, this dis-memberment of what we thought we were, is the precise – warmed by truth – process needed in order to re-member who we have always been and are still meant to be.

Old concepts of self are worth losing. These concepts lodged deeply in the unconscious, and often shared collectively, they are foundational and they follow the same course of the universe – in darkness, where the sun's energy still, always, reaches, transformation brings new life. In fact, without the dark phase of stuff breaking down, things would NOT grow. Our every personal conception happens in very warm darkness. Most creation myths begin in the dark void. Much of healing is the same.

Survivors of personal trauma often find ways to hold onto the old, or onto the decaying process itself: guilt perhaps, shame, confusion, addictions, rage, despair, all the places of very few helpful definitions of self...are clung to - rather than assuming the courage to grow new. But we can face the remember-ment. And many do thrive in the ensuing confusion. It is not unlike chaos theory – which assumes an essential order WITHIN the chaos.

"The moment you come to trust chaos, you see god clearly. Chaos is divine order, versus human order. Change is divine order, versus human order. When the chaos becomes safety to you, then you know you are seeing God clearly." (Carolyn Myss)

How do we see clearly? We let ourselves be what we are, and we feel it, embrace it, in our bodies. For there, within us, the core remains, and is always fed by ongoing light passing through. Where we find the unloved within us, we turn to love. When we find the abandoned part of us, we invite her or him back home and accept them. What has seemed to be death and decay, everything breaking down, we warm and hold and let things grow.

Rainer Maria Rilke invites this acceptance of what is and describes the need to be here clearly in his poem, "Let This Darkness Be a Bell Tower."

Let This Darkness Be A Bell Tower
Quiet friend who has come so far,
Feel how your breathing makes more space around you.
Let this darkness be a bell tower
And you the bell. As you ring,
What batters you becomes your strength.
Move back and forth into the change.
What is it like, such intensity of pain?

If the drink is bitter, turn yourself into wine.

In this uncontainable night,

Be the mystery at the crossroads of your sense,

The meaning discovered there.

And if the world ceased to hear you,

Say to the silent earth: I flow.

To the rushing water, speak: I am.

In an earlier chapter I referred to a time in my life of what seemed like utter and complete breakdown. Many years later I can see clearly, it was the necessary time of breakthrough. It plunged me into several years of discovering what lay beneath the surface, what unconscious biddings I was living by, what needed transformation and transmutation. Abandoned parts of my being I did not even know existed, I had to meet, greet, thank, and welcome home. It was not easy. It was worth every tear.

Healing work means truly diving deep. As we delve in to the compost of our own lives changing, then we can also find the inner warmth, the energy of light that is ALSO deep within and constantly moving through us from without (Consider again the number of light particles from the sun that have passed through you while reading this chapter.) There is always light, and the darkness cannot overcome it.

I once worked at a spirituality and pottery center. I learned the art of Raku. An ancient Japanese tradition, Raku is a specific process of clay work which involves radical transformations between dark and light, hot and cold. The results are that amazing crackled white glaze on black clay. Raku is often translated "crisis as opportunity." That is how I understand the process of breakdown and the metaphor of compost for healing.

"They tried to bury us. They did not realize we are seeds."
(Mexican Proverb)

Affirmations:

There is light always coming into me and through me.

Deep inside my being my fears are breaking down.

My body, mind and spirit - my soul – all work together to care for what needs caring, to guide me and to strengthen my path from the dark churning and into a new day.

I am courageous. I am strong enough.

When I reach up and out of hard times, I can see with new eyes.

I trust the process

Possible questions to ask:

If some aspect of my trauma experience and my healing is so much like the process of compost, then what does that mean? Can I observe and feel each phase in my body?

Am I afraid of breaking down? What about breaking down in front of someone else? Are there some habits I have, or some beliefs I have about myself that I could prepare for compost? Can I wait long enough to see the fruits of the hard work?

Ideas for more on these themes:

-Learn about composting and do it. Do it meditatively. Do it as a mirror of your own workings, and to care for the earth.

-Learn about Raku and find a way to experience this process.

-see You Tube: Jill Bolte Taylor Ted Talk "The Stroke of Insight."

-read Joanna Macey's translation of Rainer Maria Rilke's poetry.

Creative Non-violence connection:

In the history of creative non-violence, millions of people have been willing to lose their way of life, or their lives, for the cause. Billions of others have lived with less oppression and more freedom and dignity because of this fact.

HUMMINGBIRD. Watercolor on paper.

Hummingbird: The Power of Small

If the sun were the size of a beach ball, then Jupiter would be the size of a golf ball and the earth would be the size of a pea.

There is nothing new about the old proverb that a journey of a thousand miles begins with one small step. We hear things like this constantly. One step at a time. Honor the little things. Don't forget to stop and smell the flowers. Yada Yada .... Sometimes we use the same words or ideas so often and easily, they get old and lose their original power and meaning.

Yet, when we are looking at embracing a path of healing, all these axioms are pretty important – because some days, some hours, some minutes, all the big stuff falls apart and you just have to clean your room. Still, this chapter is NOT about the same old message. I want to add a new piece – and the teacher here is the hummingbird. As a metaphor for how healing works, the hummingbird embodies the essence of tiny acts at a time, yet something else subtly important as well. Their amazing talents and qualities are not unique *in spite* of their size... but BECAUSE of their size. Their tiny acts are huge.

Were you aware that of the 325 plus Hummingbird species, the very tiniest ones are also regarded as some of the very most fierce of all birds, regularly attacking (not just defending themselves) jays, crows, hawks, cats, dogs, people (not to mention each other), constantly. Hummingbirds are the only bird known that can sustain long term hovering, can literally fly backward, change direction almost instantaneously, and stop instantly. They are capable of up to 30mph flying forward and up to 60mph in a dive. Some can achieve up to 10g's executing a courtship dive. (Trained fighter pilots are lucky to do 9gs in a dive or hard turn.) Their travel speed relative to size is faster than the space shuttle re-entering our atmosphere. The Rufus Hummingbird makes a 3,000-mile trip from Alaska and Southern California to Mexico, and back. The Ruby Red Throat crosses the 500-mile Gulf of Mexico nonstop 2x every year. They average 1,200 heart beats and 250 breaths per minute and 50-200 wing flaps per second (depending on direction and air conditions). Those little tongues are like mini pumps and can drain a flower in less than a second. You think they are just flitting from one flower to another like they can't make up their mind? No, they are efficiently draining some or all from each plant faster than you can see it.

These gorgeous birds of smallness seem to revel and peak in who they are and how they are made. And we love them for it. We love their song, their zooming around, their beautiful colors and sparkles, the fact that we aren't actually able to SEE them in full flight (we just know we've been buzzed,) and how they accent a flower garden. Hummingbirds are also vital for pollination - hence plant growth and the food we put on our dinner table.

It would be easy to say that the lesson we have from the hummer is the importance of small things, small steps. Supposedly it was Van Gogh who said, "Great things are done by a series of small steps put together." **But** there are at least two reasons why that is NOT the only or the main lesson to be gleaned from this tiny teacher.

First, it seems to me that way too often the whole theme of little steps can become like a burden. This can be exacerbated by doctors, psychiatrists, therapists, even other survivors, certainly general society, pushing people to do the necessary stuff. Gain the cognitive behavioral discipline and keep moving!

This is with the view that where you are now (just taking steps) is not ok *enough*. You are supposed to be GETTING somewhere else, over there. In this light, each small step is a burden or a necessary evil. It's hard to do. In fact it's easy to hate the little steps now when we only have our eyes on something "bigger and better" a whole lot of steps away. These kinds of steps are like stairs, always going up (or down). Always climbing, or falling back and having to climb again, is draining, tiring, takes a lot of work, depends on discipline and long vision. To be honest, taking steps like these is just not very gratifying: not inwardly, the deep healing kind of gratifying. It is easy to feel depressed when all the little steps just feel like work. Will I ever get THERE?

The second reason we do not have to focus on "small steps" is more fun and includes a little basic science. Remember, Hummingbird is the metaphor, the teacher. Well, guess what? Hummingbirds do not take steps. Literally. They cannot walk. They can sit. They fly. They hover and dive and sometimes sort of hop. But they cannot walk. They do not take steps of any kind. They ACT. And as tiny little beings, their actions are huge.

Hummingbirds embody vitality – the potential ENERGY involved - in BEING small, and therefore accomplish what NO OTHER BIRD OR ANIMAL OR PERSON is capable of doing. This teacher says that the greatest potential energy we know of is in the tiniest thing. (Nuclear fusion anyone?)

In healing work, it is much the same. Each tiny act carries energy. Each tiny release of energy provides a sense of accomplishment. And each accomplishment provides a sense of well-being, or at least *better-being*. And the experiences of better being and well- being lead us to want more, so motivation to DO more grows. **This is subtle and important**. The small act is not about trying to someday get somewhere else. The small act is in itself FUELING further movement and is wonderful all by itself. DO I know where next? Maybe not. But I have the energy to go.

Consider all those facts about what Hummers are actually capable of...things that larger birds (or people) can NOT do, in fact no other animal on earth can do. What is it about SMALL that makes for SO MUCH ENERGY? So much potential? WHY is the mustard seed used as a metaphor? WHY do we refer to the acorn and its potential? WHY is contemporary physics researching and experimenting with the tiniest (unseen by the human eye) levels of existence (quarks and beyond) --- and discovering unimaginable (before) sources of energy? In all cases, the potential energy is not *in spite* of smallness, but *because* of it. There is something about the compression of energy into the smallest things, once released, being the source of seemingly unstoppable energy. This means something for trauma and healing work.

Trauma can be described as stuck energy - stuck in the body. All these unfinished emotions attached to the difficult event become compressed into our body: in our muscles and joints, our gut, everywhere. If it sits there without release for too long, it can cause all kinds of physical troubles, which then work on our mind and spirit. So, release is important. But if you release it too fast, it can become overwhelming. Peter Levine speaks both of pendulation (moving in and out of the releasing energy) and titration (releasing only small amounts at a time) as vital tools for releasing the energy wisely. As I imagine a hummingbird hovering, zooming, stopping, diving, zooming, sitting, hovering, zooming, in all directions too fast for my eye to catch, I think maybe the hummingbird has mastered both. For those of us in healing work, it takes a great deal of careful attention and awareness to pendulate in and out, appreciate each action, and feel it in our bodies well enough and soon enough to be able to titrate the exponential energy. Awareness and observation are key. They work like mindfulness, watching ourselves move, intensely paying attention to what is going on in the body. It can be sort of like awe, to pay such careful attention.

This concept is at the heart of meditation, the core of mindfulness, the power of non-violence, and a lot of current quantum physics. The more attentive and consciously present we are to each moment and every small act, the more these moments and acts release their exponential energy into the rest of our lives. We don't have to WORK at it. It simply IS how things work.

A similar process is observable in the chambered nautilus. One chamber at a time is PART of the picture. But for our point, it is the fact that the nautilus gives full attention to one chamber at a time that the next chamber is already prepared when it is time to grow on. When a young nautilus first hatches from its egg it is about an inch in diameter and has a shell with seven small chambers. As it drifts about feeding on plankton and other tiny prey, the animal grows until it completely fills one chamber, while the next one is being built – just a bit larger than the last – ready for growth. At the precise moment needed, the animal moves into the next chamber and the process starts again. It grows until it is "done" with that chamber before moving on. Metaphorically, BECAUSE it is mindful of where it is, honoring the one space in its growth at a time, the NEXT space is already, by design, being prepared. Being fully present to one act, releases the energy needed for the next. When it is time to grow again, what is needed is already in place. In other words, the mindfulness of NOW is the force which creates the future, without worry or planning. Growth simply happens most smoothly in that way. Again, do I KNOW where to next, or what? Maybe not. And maybe I don't need to. I have what it takes.

Coming back to the hummingbird, there is yet another lovely metaphor applicable to healing. Relative to the size of its body, the hummingbird has the largest brain of any other bird, and one of the very largest hearts. Most of those tiny bodies flitting around your garden are made up of brain and heart. The other organs are miniscule, and some we might expect are simply non-existent, so the animal has unique adaptions. Perhaps because the tiny bird is so packed with exponential energy, the mind and the heart HAVE to be the biggest organs at work. To me this fact speaks to the need for self-compassion.

When we have pent up energies because of past (and present) trauma, it is acts of self-compassion which are needed to care for the self, not let the energies stay stuck, not let the energies become overwhelming. Self-compassion is a capacity we experience when our mind and heart are focused and working as one. If we could live this way all the time, our bodies metaphorically full of mind and heart as one, largest in our awareness, I think maybe the world would be a much happier place. Certainly, we would be happier. Perhaps it is no accident that in many indigenous traditions, the hummingbird is the symbol for joy.

There are many ways to "be here now" which enable the constant movement of the universe and beyond. There are innumerable ways to honor the healing path NOW, slowly and in a way which provides more energy just by doing it. The present potential …. Is everything. Being present, to the present small moment, automatically adds a healing balm or salve on the past and provides the energy and space for what is needed in the future.

"Start with what is necessary, then do what is possible and soon you will be doing the impossible." (Francis of Assisi)

Affirmations:

I can start now. I will honor the smallest acts of the day.

The smallest act I do, in a present way, sources everything else.

I am small and I am powerful.

My mind and my heart are one.

I pendulate. I easily move in and out of my healing release of energy.

I allow just enough release at a time to observe and stand in awe of my body and the process of healing.

Possible questions to ask:

If some of my healing work is so much the same as the hummingbird, what does that mean? Can I observe and feel the different actions of the hummingbird in my own body? Can I appreciate each small act I choose this day, and harness the energy?

Can I practice self-compassion, letting the unity of my heart and mind be first in my healing work? Do I judge myself for not getting somewhere else fast enough? Do I believe I need to be overwhelmed to have proof that healing is happening, or that something happened in the past? Can I let go of those judgments and stand in awe and gratitude instead? How can I learn more about mindfulness? Do I sometimes feel that intensive energy in my body and yet do not give it compassionate attention?

For more on these themes:

- plant seeds for flowers that hummingbirds love and need.

- learn about the trillions upon trillions of neurons, synapses and atoms at work in your brain, in your hands and in the book you are reading. They are working.

- research what nuclear fusion is and how it works.

-when you are washing dishes, look for rainbows in the suds.

-Be mindful of what you are doing right at that moment and notice your energy level change.

- watch a you tube video of the development of a fetus, from one cell. Stop it now and then and stare. Consider how important each minute is.

-reassess what the mustard seed metaphor is all about. Consider newly the potential energy alive in the tiny acorn.

- love hummingbirds. Plant flowers they love.

NON-VIOLENCE connection:

Nonviolence is often not about seeing any immediate results. It is a way of being and a process which relies upon the power and energy of each tiny seemingly unimportant, seemingly ineffective, mindful act coming from the power within.

"I was once spiritually ill -we all pass through that – but one day the intelligence of my soul cured me." (Meister Eckhart)

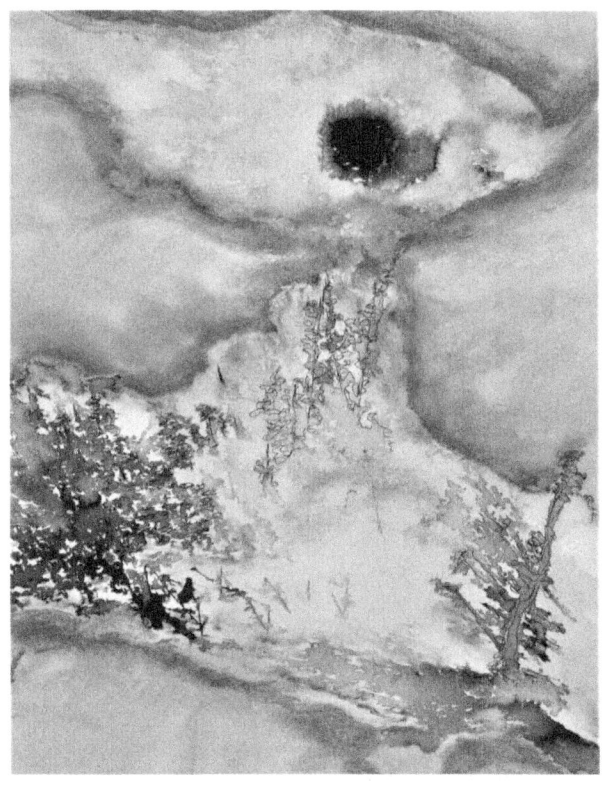

THE SPACE BETWEEN. Watercolor and ink on paper.

Waves: The Space Between

Every 11 years, the magnetic poles of the sun switch.

This process is called Solar Max.

I was a very young child when I first experienced the vast open sky and long, long walks on the beach of the Pacific Ocean. It was a place of safety for me, splashing in the shallows, sitting and watching the coming and going, closing my eyes and feeling the warm sand and salty air. It is an experience of forever hearing that which is constant: a sound that comes and goes, a feeling that pulls and pushes, and space in between.

Anyone who has walked along a coastline knows this experience of the waters coming in and pulling away. These waves are caused mostly by the friction of wind on top of the water pushing down, or over the top pushing sideways. What is underneath, however, the silent and deep ocean, is not water moving in and out. Instead, through the silent water, energy is being held and energy is moving through. It APPEARS to us as though the ocean is moving forward and back but in truth only a very small amount of water is doing that, right on the top of things.

Water is a flexible medium. The molecules absorb the energy around them. So, when the earth moves in a different way - the constantly moving tectonic plates below the sea, faulting sea floors, volcanic eruptions above and below the waters, or something moving IN water such as whales or titanic boats, great schools of marine life - the energy caused by the movement is absorbed by the water molecules. The energy moves THROUGH the water. In open ocean, without much wind, this looks like great rounded swells, and is actually the energy moving in circular patterns below the surface. On top, with enough wind, we see the waves.

    We know that waves have peaks and troughs, highs and lows, and they travel in groups, wave-trains, with spaces of calm between. These gusts of energy then "break" upon the edges, the cliffs and beaches, or rush forward into rivers. We then call this movement, waves. But really it is just the top being blown around. Rivers flow downward into the ocean and that water either moves deeply downward, or dissipates along the top, depending on the geography. Waves pushed by wind may travel seemingly inland, but the larger undercurrent is always TOWARD the deep ocean. That is a poetic reality. And it is true unless the energy is so huge that for a short period of time it moves upwards into rivers and over land, meaning a tsunami. But even the tremendous tsunami recedes and the waters resume their deep circulation, and topside waves.

It fascinates me that what I see on the surface, is in fact only the surface. The waves at the beach do not reflect what is going on in the depths. They may seem tumultuous, while underneath there is calm. They may seem calm even when underneath there is a tsunami on its way.

Sound like healing work? I know within my own journey that sometimes my greatest calm and quiet is when the deepest most grueling work is going on. I also know that in my day to day goings on, sometimes the rants and drama are only on the surface. The surface is often just the surface, important and changeable if we want, and less necessary to our being over time. I think the deeper truth of who we are is like the deep ocean: constant and vast, able to support life, and made to allow waves of energy to move through. Emotions are waves of energy and our bodies are created to allow them through.

"I am not my present reality; I am my truth."   African proverb

This deep undercurrent is quite often the true emotion we carry. Emotion is energy which moves through us, through the matter and the water of our physical being, through our psyche like deep tides, and sometimes like little waves blown by the wind. Being committed to the healing path means being committed to the deep tides and accepting the surface stuff as surface stuff. If we cannot feel the undercurrent, we see only a series of things splashing, going and coming again – and often, again. This is being blown about, without much control, at the whim of big and small winds from all directions. What is needed is some kind of connection to the deep and abiding depths, the swells, the circular patterns, the abundance, the inner power.

Sometimes the source of the deep movement, these deep feelings, is held at bay from us. We call it the unconscious or the subconscious. But it is that which moves in us most profoundly.

Is it all hidden from us? I prefer to imagine that what seems hidden is only contained: held in a vast open space within, our un-met emotion moves and has its being. It is all held, as in a womb space, waiting its proper time to show and be named - to be MET. "Hello old feeling set aside, held deeply within all this time. How are you today?"

Deep emotion is difficult. It is the sudden choking up when you mention a person's name who you have loved and miss. It is the wracking grief, the silent shock, the unending tears. It is the justice and rage when from your truth when you know something is wrong, off, unjust – whether or not you can put it into words. It is the tension in your chest, your head, your fist. It is your inability to speak, coupled with the desperate need to speak. It is the unmet injustice in the world around us, too.

Within our emotional well is our wisdom, our PERSONAL wisdom. It is mine or it is yours, through my life circumstances or yours, and our own ways of learning. It is a tremendous gift to share our true emotional self, and to have someone else share theirs with us. It is a gift to cry for the world.

To meet ourselves in our deep tides is to become the hero of our own story again and again – and when we can do that, then we have something to share. We don't have the answers for anyone else. We have OUR answers, from OUR experience and OUR wisdom. If every single being could share precisely that, and only that, then we would have **that many answers** and all of them would be true. There is no one right way for growing or for healing. There is only your way. These are the only gifts we truly own and can truly, freely, give. When we share our personal stories, and the depth of feelings, we share from our own experience and find that while the experience is different, the WAY emotions move, like energy in the deep sea, is similar. The ever-flowing constant depths, we have in common.

"You didn't come into this world. You came 'out 'of it, like a wave from the ocean. You are not a stranger here." (Allan Watts)

So here we are, born out of deep truth, full of deep emotion and dreams, and often still all thrown about on the surface and at the edges – so to speak – where we "break" day by day, minute by minute.

We walk in these waves and between them as they come and as they go. We suffer them sometimes. We kick and splash. We want them to stop coming. We don't want them to just go away. We observe how the landscape changes with each wave. And we learn to watch, hopefully, knowing there is more to the picture, trusting the deep-ness nearby. Just a short distance away, the depths of holding remain.

"Energy flows, out and in, everything has its tides; all things rise and fall, the pendulum swing manifests in everything . . . rhythm compensates. . . . " *(from the mystical text of the Hermetic Kybalion)*

Trauma seems to collide with the natural rhythm. Rather than being part of the natural under currents, trauma causes a stopping of energy, a stop to the natural ever-flowing of life. It is a sudden disruption once, or many times over. Or it is a sudden overwhelm which stops us. Either way, Survivors of childhood traumas walk around in bodies that have not been able to finish the circular patterning. Survivors of our daily global traumas walk around unrepaired as well, overwhelmed and without enough common supports. The deep energy is not able to move through to completion.

Up on the surface? It's a mess being blown about and stuck there. It's reactionary. It may be in fight or flight or freeze or collapse. It may be dazed and in shock, or ranting, or depressed every other day or manic. Parts of the self are stuck. Parts of our WHOLENESS are not flowing, not being part of continuing growth. Healing is about changing this. It is about gradually allowing the stuck stuff to flow through, to finish the natural cycle in the deepest areas of our sea. It is about gradually allowing everyone a common shift, a trembling we all share to calm again. "Gradual" is an important word because it is not a simple task to go from stuck to unstuck. The nervous system swings back and forth because it needs to do that. Grief comes in waves because that is what is natural, that is how things work. It is our job to trust this. "Rhythm compensates."

This is a lovely sentence and true. Yes, we have ups and downs in life, or every day, back and forth sometimes every hour. But the fact that this rhythm exists, by itself, reminds us that we can continue. The pendulum will keep swinging. We can choose to be with it, or to fight against it.

"Every trauma provides an opportunity for authentic transformation. Trauma amplifies and evokes the expansion and contraction of psyche, body and soul. It is how we respond to a traumatic event that determines where trauma will be a cruel and punishing Medusa turning us into stone, or whether it will be a spiritual teacher taking us along vast and uncharted pathways."
(Peter Levine)

There are so many different waves, and many possibilities. We can choose one, and then another, and more keep coming. There is no way to stand within only one truth as it breaks upon our shores. We walk between them, and hopefully without bias. We do not have to have a bias for light over dark, happiness over sadness, joy over sorrow, a bias even for health over illness or one-ness over multiplicity. We can walk between and hold them **all** as they come and go. The deep truth within which bears where we came from, allows us the same fluidity required to stay in the tension of opposites, the give and take of difference.

"Being and non-being create each other/ difficult and easy support each other/ long and short define each other/ before and after follow each other." (Tao Te Ching 2)

Carl Jung wrote extensively about the balancing of opposites. The shadow must become conscious (into the light) to heal and be made whole. The anima and animus need to understand each other and work together. The Yin and Yang know each other intimately.

"To know wholeness we must dance the opposites." (Joan Borysenko)

To dance is to know the steps, to practice the ins and outs, the thrusts and the absolute necessity of pause. Music reflects the same pattern of ups and downs and thrusts, and absolutely depends on the precise pause. Imagine walking on a beach again. Sometimes, the wave that just went past soaks back into sand, or dries, slightly before the next wave arrives. Sometimes the last one that went back home seems to hold on a long time before another one comes. There is just sand, or water not really moving in or out, but stillness. There is a moment of no movement, a quieting. Sometimes as we watch the water and sand, the same thing happens inside: a quieting.

While we are doing healing work, or just handling the traumas of life, these moments of rest between the forever coming and forever going are essential. When it is emotion that is coming in wave trains, like grief does, those moments between are like chocolate. Taste it and take it in, relish the calm because the next wave will in fact arrive. It will still be your teacher, no matter what feelings are brought, and the calm between is a teacher too.

Imagine the waves as past and future. In the center place between, you are not only a part of your past history, but also a part of your future. The calm between is a be-here-now moment. The center is where we can be open to no-particular-outcome. We can be ready for what comes without passive waiting *and* without forcing anything. It is the place to remember there is more to come, always, while remembering where we have been. It is the place to open new doors consciously – like those next waves (they are coming anyway!) It is easier, smoother, to be aware. The pauses help us to watch the changes leaving and wait for the changes coming.

"To hope means to be ready at every moment for that which is not yet born." (Erich Fromm)

I think that hope is like the "rest" in a musical piece. It is essential --- otherwise every song would just be ongoing noise. Hope in healing work is the same: a kind of rest so that the work is not just constant noise.

I still am in love with the experience of walking along the edge of ocean, in the waves. It is a place I find myself being very present. I lose track of troubles in the mind, things that are bothering me, stuff I am supposed to get done. I find a very present presence – and this teacher helps me everywhere else I go. I currently live in the mountains and only get to walk a beach about once a year. But I do not forget it. The memory is vivid and visceral. That may seem strange, to remember being present viscerally. But it is tactile memory – I hold it in my bones (that is how memory works) - and it is so complete and enjoyable, it invites me to be more present everywhere else.

As a survivor of trauma, I also know that sometimes being present in that space between means holding the ambiguity and confusion. When much of life is portrayed as polar opposites, holding the space between is a true and honest challenge, and one which mindfulness to NOW can help us to choose, and teach us how. We do not have to be washed over by one side or another. We can embrace each, and still hold the space between with compassion and generosity and curiosity. Our trauma filled world needs us to choose this way of being, and our conscious sacred healing work is a teacher.

"As sensitive human beings, we may often be asked to meet very vivid waves of emotion and sensation in our bodies and in our tender hearts. When we learn to stay with our present experience – rather than engage in habitual responses of fight, flight or freeze – and start to bring acceptance and kindness into these waves, we may discover that they are not harming us." (Matt Licatta)

Affirmations:

My deepest natural rhythms are in sync with the universe and taking care of me.

The waves of grief will not last. I can care for myself between them. I can appreciate the coming and going and the pausing.

I get to choose. I can kick and splash. I can wade slowly. I can stand still. I can marvel. I can go sit on the beach for a while. I can dance.

My emotions are real and true and deserve their space. I am learning to finish the cycles and restore balance.

I can hold the space between opposites. I fill the gap with compassion.

Possible questions to ask:

If my experience of trauma and healing is so much like the experience of waves and their coming and going and pausing, what does that mean? Can I feel these movements in my body?

Am I holding on too tightly to one thing or another? Am I freezing or running away or collapsing rather than allowing the waves and resting in the pause? What is it I need in order to start the flow again? Who can help me remember? Do I trust my emotions? Are these emotions from the past, or are they present, or some of both? How am I doing with self care? Can I be compassionate when I experience polar opposites in myself, in others, in society? Can I be a bridge by being in my center?

For more on these themes:

-Look up almost anything by Peter Levine.

-consider learning more yoga, for rest periods and for slowing down.

-learn to breathe deeply. Deep full breath is compassion through waves of grief.

-Keep a journal and track your feelings in a day, in an hour. Can you see the pendulum at times?

-Remember that Grief is a way of enlightenment. Deep emotions are the way of belonging to the natural cycles of the universe.

-Google Pema Chodron's video on living with vulnerability.

-Sing a lot and pay attention to the vital pause in your breath and body, in the lyrics, in the meaning.

-Research the Polyvagal Theory.

Non-violent connection:

Non-violent action and way of life is about standing in the gap between polarities. It is a commitment to holding many realities at once and honoring them all because they all hold truth.

Nature teaches us these things.

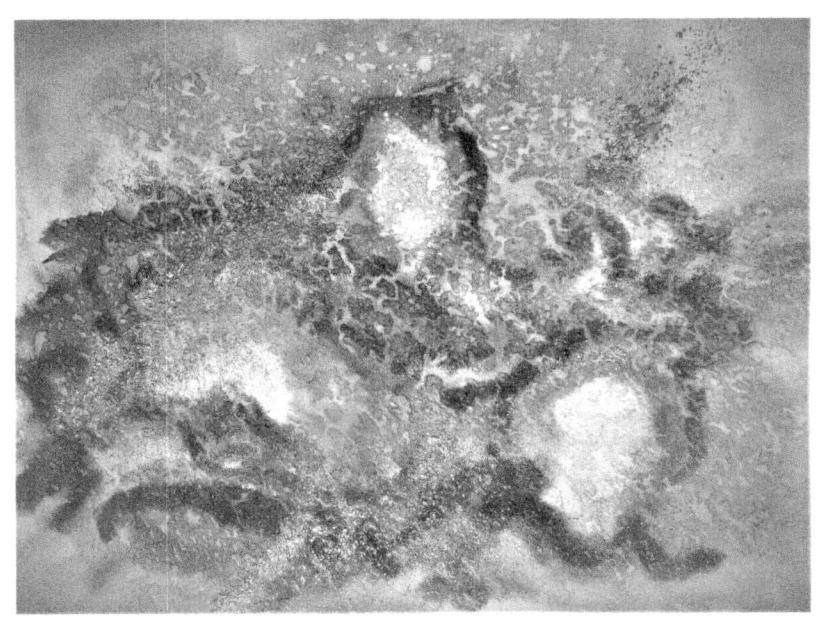

INNER FIRE. Watercolor and glitter on paper.

Embers: Things Which Remain

It takes 50 million years for the energy produced at the core of the sun to reach its surface and then race to the earth. If the sun suddenly stopped producing energy, it would take another 50 billion years for the earth to take notice.

It is an enduring image, filled with the smells, the temperature, the time of day, maybe the place and other people gathered: sitting around a campfire or in front of a fireplace looking long into the embers. Time seems to go away and the lingering warmth and light make us go into a soul place, a place of things important. How many humans and other animals throughout all ages have sat and stared into the embers? What mirror is there in the embers, what do we see with our eyes that resonates deeply in our bodies and souls?

Embers are generally defined as the small pieces of glowing coal or wood in a dying fire. They are also, "glowing bits of leftover fire which can re-ignite." A suggested synonym is "live coal." So metaphorically speaking, being part of something dying while also having the potential to be re-born, is to be "alive."

"Perhaps we are all scintillae: the fiery sparks of soul stuff, the light of nature, the luminous spheres in a deepening/darkening soul..." (Janet O' Dallet)

As I prepared to write this chapter I sat long with several different possible themes, different aspects of healing that can bear us up for a long time, seen or unseen. I thought of the different kinds of memory from all the senses, suppressed memory, body memory, unconscious memory – things that can suddenly ignite and BE seen, things inside which stay, which help to warm and light our way whether or not we know they are even there. I thought of difficult memories, traumatic memory, things that seem to be there but only as part of something dying and broken down. It took a lot of time. I mulled over each of them as if I were in fact sitting before a driftwood fire on the beach, in the dark, with the added sound of waves and ocean salt in the air, warm sand. I chose a few that I think challenge us, invite us to tend the fire that might need re-igniting.

Tending the fire means finding the embers that still do exist and then carefully and knowingly providing what is needed to help them re-ignite and burn more strongly, be seen, heard, known, felt. Tending the fire means making sure that everyone sitting around stays warm, that the sacred space continues (think yule log and sanctuary flames), that all who long to be in that place of no-time-just-being, can be in that place. Tending to the fire means knowing what is needed and providing it - just the right extra bit of breath blown, the right tinder to add in just the right way, some sculpting of new wood for the continuing dance of flames, shovel of dirt over here, moving rocks around over there - whatever is needed. Tending the fire also means moving close and being vulnerable to a stray spark or a simple brushing near and getting burnt. This experience is also an important way to learn what to avoid and what to do next time. The possibility of fire brings light, warmth, protection and danger. How and why we tend to the embers, makes all the difference. My chosen themes are embers of healing that require attention: need, shame, the inner spark, self-compassion. It is time to tend these slow fires.

Traumatic events going unresolved can in fact make us avoid or deny all of these. We fear getting burnt again and neglect our needs or even stop needing, stop feeling that feeling.

We doubt our worth and limit ourselves. We can feel so burned and fallen apart that we doubt any little spark is left, or that it is enough to re-ignite. We neglect or deny or avoid our pain and therefore do not practice self-compassion. If we stop here, though, we miss out on all the light, warmth and protection, the life-giving vitality of embers and fires. We miss the alchemy involved, the homeopathic natural state of being our own best medicine – at our best AND our worst.

"Mercurius, the revelatory light of nature is also hell-fire, which in some miraculous way is none other than the rearrangement of the heavenly, spiritual powers in the lower, chthonic world of matter." (Carl Jung in "Alchemical Studies" volume 13 of Collected Works)

When we are born, we are so terribly vulnerable, in tremendous need. What sustained us for almost ten months has disappeared via a harsh struggle into an entirely foreign environment. But, because we have experienced the gentle watery womb, this sudden, new sense of need comes right alongside of deep expectancy. Somewhere inside as infants we simply KNOW that our needs will be provided for, as they should be. For the most part, in **natural** circumstances, this has been our experience so far. Why would it not continue? That is part of the miracle of becoming. We EXPECT, and discover with joy, that what we need to continue will be given. We cry and someone holds us, feeds us, cares. We reach out and someone holds us. We try new things and discover everything with a sense of joy, and others are there to celebrate each and every new step.

However, trauma is not natural. So, I think that many survivors of trauma (especially childhood) end up uncomfortable or practically hating the sensation of need. Our natural expectations were unheeded or used against us. Neglected or abused, no one noticed the little light was going out. Somewhere along the way we learned to set aside the joyful expectancy, just put it away and not feel the need we still indeed had. Somewhere along the way once, or many times over, those who were part of our natural order of becoming did not do their job. They did not meet us and see us and hear us and give what we sought and wanted and deserved. And that hurt caused a shutdown of hope, a closing off of expectant joy, an inability to get all creative and have fun discovering how to ask and how to receive everything – literally everything – with hope and joy. *Gleeful lack of control* became something not to be trusted any more. All of this is true as we adults clamor to figure out our needs and the needs of all in a world of global turmoil and disconnection.

But need is a basic instinct for survival and becoming and continuing. It is MEANT to be coupled with expectant joy and hope and discovery and creativity. It is meant to be a door, a sacred door of connection. *Seek and you will find. Knock and the door will be opened.*

It is trauma, and maybe in particular the betrayal kind, that couples need with things like fear and loss, hurt, pain, inability to reach out, isolation, helplessness. If as adults all our minds and bodies can bring us when we feel need is all of that???

When we think of being needy or dependent, we risk an anxiety attack? No wonder we fight it! No wonder it is so hard. To consider trusting in the natural way of being again scares us into the old experiences of having it all shattered, and we close up again and say no. No I do not want to feel that. No I will not take that risk. No I do not need. No I don't even want.

We begin to believe that is easier to not need, but when the spark is too cold and too dim, that risk is about dying. Suddenly we have become cold and realize it is time to tend the fire. Sometimes when it seems all the light is gone, we realize we still want life, still want to find the inner fire, still want to discover and grow. Get up and tend to the embers.

It is like sitting before the glowing coals. We recognize something and we still wish for more, for deep light, deep safety, deep warmth, the creative dancing of flames. We still WISH for the joyful freedom of expectancy and discovery and having needs met because there is still a fire burning, a real one, a natural one, the truth that when those things went so wrong we deserved to be cared for. In the natural world, need isn't actually about absence. It is about searching with trust. The answer is already here somewhere. We look for ways to re-MEMBER, to seek and find, knock and find the door open, ask and receive, need and have someone be there.

"When god had made (the man) he made him all out of stuff that sung all the time and glittered all over. Some angels got jealous and chopped him into a million pieces, but still he glittered and hummed. So they beat him down to nothing but sparks but each little spark had a shine and a song. So they covered each one with mud. And the lonesomeness in the sparks made them hunt for one-another." (Anna in, <u>Mr. God, This is Anna</u> by Fynn)

Choosing to heal is when we know we need to tend to our hurt, and often it comes to us as we experience those embers at the very bottom of the pile. The fine wood limbs and trunks have all broken away, fallen open, become tiny little piece barely warm, barely lit stuff, on the ground - and under the pile, is need.

Feeling shattered like that, all broken up in pieces, having the original innocence and original dream broken up viscerally, is one definition of shame. Shame is visceral. It is in the body, in the wood of our being, in our bones. It shows up in that instant body recognition that things are not right, and it turns into "I" am not right because of words that usually belong to other people, words of abusers and other ignorant folk. Feeling need is not supposed to be like that. It is not supposed to be about shame. Feeling need is normal and natural. And when we find the right relationships – friends, partners, therapists, children, trees, boulders, water …. we allow the need to again be coupled with expectant joy, which is also visceral. Your whole body shakes in excitement and change. Old cells fly off like ashes, and new tiny fires ignite and fill the air with sparks, and your whole being glows. Like it is supposed to. Like it does because it is part of creation. Creation where everything shines. Creation which can make no mistakes.

We are embers, and we have embers of truth within, and we need each other to tend each other. We are like stars, stars whose light shines long and bright to remind us of the original beauty. Like embers in the night sky.. .. What is most true and real, remains to light our way.

"When I have an idea, I turn down the flame ...as low as it will go. Then it explodes and that is my idea." (Earnest Hemmingway)

We tend to get very creative when we must endure, when trauma of some kind threatens our being. We do what needs doing. If that means keeping one piece of coal hidden but alive within the deadened fire, then we do it. We hide it from the elements. We keep it warm. Hopefully we do not forget it is there, ready to spark when it is time, when safety invites new life and new beauty and new warmth. These are important acts. Tending to that hidden coal, tending the low fires, is a creative way to re-member. We have all sorts of rituals for this - meditation, gardening, romance, exercise and yoga, spiritual rituals, baking with a child, volunteering and feeling good about helping others, hiking, building cairns, doing art ... rituals that bring us home, that re-ignite the long-hidden. These are acts of self-compassion, ways of caring for what is still true – the holy spark and the sacred song.

"Ritual is called for because the soul communicates things to us that the body translates as need, or want, or absence. So we enter into ritual to respond to the call of the soul...." (Malidome)

Rituals of self-compassion are not necessarily easy when times have been hard, or are hard now. We have forgotten how and when we try, the muscle memory seems lost. How do we do this? Why is it so hard? Are we worth all this struggle? Perhaps we forgot where the rest of the wood even is? How to chop wood and carry water. Where is the trowel? How hard do I blow and where? I can't bend down that far. The city won't let me build a fire. Sometimes – often times with trauma – what is long-hidden is what hurts the most. Even though these things are the harbingers of new life for us, even though they are the seeds we need to flower, they also hurt. I think maybe it takes a great deal of energy for a small ember on a dying log to garner all it needs to spark again. It is tiring and we get tired. (picture someone blowing hard on an almost spent chunk of wood with only tiny bits of warm ember left.) Sometimes "tending" forces it, like burn scars that must be torn away over and over again until the clean flesh again grows well. So it hurts. It is hard work. It can burn to heal.

Old fears, old pain, old betrayal, old hurts, neglect… why would we want to go there??? But these things we hide away are because they are like children, little sparks of life. They are infant and young tender parts of us who need a home – our home. They need to grow. We need to tend to them. They are our fire. My hurt child screaming to be seen, carries my wisdom. I need her fire to carry on. And I need her fire to rem-ember that I am not alone. We gather around fires because there we know we are not alone. This is ancient ritual, ancient gathering, ancient truth.

The world is on fire

Let the embers warm and keep us

Let the embers ignite and call us to gather more

While they break down and transform what is no longer needed in the same way

Let the lingering light shine deep into the night

And warm us still

When day breaks open

And the larger Fire reminds us

"I am with you"

ARW 2016

Affirmations:

I am the power that hid and protected my inner fire.

I will let my light shine.

What I need to tend the old fires is available to me.

I am compassionate with myself. What has been hidden I will welcome as a tiny spark waiting to be re-ignited.

Possible questions to ask:

If my experience of trauma and healing is so much like embers and the process of tending to the fire, what does that mean? Can I feel the different states of fire in my body?

How deep are my deepest needs? How do I feel them? How do I care for them? Have I forgotten them and let their fire turn to cold coals? Do I deny my needs, hate them, not even know them? Can I grieve what did NOT happen? What can I do now to more intentionally tend to my hidden, dying-out needs and desires?

Who can I get to help me gather the wood and celebrate gathering around a bonfire?

For more on these themes:

-Make a long list of what you already do to care for yourself and ask the question, "is this about now, or then?

-remember yourself as a child and spend time with the experience of longing. What did not happen? Cry.

-Look up Brene Brown, her Ted talks, books and presentations on shame.

-google a Makers video: Nadia Bolz-Weber, May of 2018, on shame.

-look up the science of fire and be in awe – feel it in your body.

-light a candle regularly.

-have a bonfire with friends and be the one who tends to the fire as it goes low. Feel how you are caring for yourself and others, bringing about the possibility of more warmth and more light.

Non-violence connection:

Non-violence is about knowing there is an inner spark, and some very hidden and forgotten, in all people. A non-violent confrontation is about tending to the spark in the self and in the "enemy."

CHIAROSCURIFY. Ink on paper.

Shadow: Teacher of Balance

Sunspots appear to be dark spots on the surface of the sun, but if the sunspot were isolated from the surrounding photosphere it would still be brighter than the moon.

Many people are familiar with the yin yang sign and some of what it means. You see a circle with one side black and one side white, and each has a smaller circle within it of the opposite color. The general idea is to remember that there is always light within darkness and darkness within light. Truly it makes little sense to speak of shadows without also speaking of light, as they illumine each other – make each other more visible and clear.

People may also be very aware of *shadow* as it is used in psychological and sociological language, as the "dark side" of a personality, the elements in our being we do not always want to "see" but which we need to acknowledge and be in relationship with to understand wholeness. This is quite helpful, as much of the healing journey is about uncovering what has been covered, bringing into light that which has been hidden.

For Carl Jung and many others, and like the yin yang symbolizes, the qualities of dark and light are not opposites, and neither needs to be considered as "good" or "bad." They are two aspects of the same ongoing truth, the same ever-flowing energy. Both/all are necessary for any and all organisms, or persons, to grow physically, psychologically and spiritually: dark/light; day/night; sleep/awake; movement/pause – all are necessary.

There are also interesting scientific facts which also have meaning metaphorically. There is such a thing as colored shadow. There are shadows made up from numerous light sources at once (rather than one light source casting a single shadow). There are temperature shadows, cold and warm. Color theory informs us that there is actually no such thing as black. Light is an energy that travels in particles and waves. Shadows are formed when some bit of this energy is blocked by something else: an opaque thing, a transparent thing, a translucent thing, another light source, heat, cold, movement. All shadows are gradient, depending on where the primary light source is, and other light sources, and movement. When you look out your window on a sunny day and see the sun on the grass and the shade under the trees, you are not seeing "black" and "white" or even much dark and light. It is all gradients of the same ever-flowing energy, variants of gray. Would that we could see each other in the same way.

Gray is where the light and dark actually share their energy. Gray points to the magic of what it means to chiaroscurofy. This is a word which means, "to find a comfortable place where you are partially illuminated in darkness and partially illuminated in lightness, or half in shadow and half in sunlight." (Rob Brezny suggests this verb for the noun chiaroscuro in, <u>Pronoia is the Antidote to Paranoia</u>)

Whenever we view our own night sky, standing in awe of the myriad stars and galaxies we cannot see otherwise, this experience is a direct result of the earth casting a shadow. Gaia turns, and blocks so much light coming from the sun that a great shadow makes our personal view of the sky *look* dark (though it has not truly changed.) And in that dark night, the tiniest pinpoints of light are revealed and we have a new understanding of our place in the universe. We stand in a different *kind* of light, less afraid, with more things illumined, seemingly dark but really quite clear. The interplay of light and dark creates a kind of numinous seeing. Stand in the dark under the stars and moon and just wait: things become very clear.

"The sun is nice but it lights things up so much that you can't see very far...the night time is better. It stretches your soul to the stars." (Anna in, <u>Mr God, this is Anna</u> by Fynn)

Carl Jung may have coined the phrase, "darkness is the great awakener" but the idea has been around forever. The Huna people, for example, *begin* their day at dusk, as the sun seems to be setting. Winter Solstice in the Northern Hemisphere is the longest, darkest day of the year, and simultaneously the beginning of Summer. The fetus begins to grow in the darkness of the womb. Seeds are planted in the dark earth. Myths of creation in myriad traditions begin in darkness. So many examples throughout the history of the planet and its people show us that light springs forth from darkness.

And yet we tend to avoid it within ourselves. Jung wrote extensively on the shadow self and defined the wholeness of Self as a relationship between the conscious and unconscious, the known and unknown, the "best" and "worst", the light and the dark of our personalities and the things which make us move. His work delved into the deep unconscious, the shared collective unconscious, things which move us to act in certain ways even though we are not yet aware of them, or do not want them to actually exist. But for Jung these were not bad monsters, but examples of archetypal patterns existing everywhere and in everything.

Most of us are a bit more superficial and just think in terms of specific traits we ARE sort of aware of but just don't like in ourselves: rage; depression; addiction; fears; confusion and "craziness"; mean-ness; jealousy; obsessions; triggered reactions; etc. Either way, the deep unconscious or the sort of avoided semi-conscious, these "shadow things" are still meant to work like the yin yang. They are part of our wholeness and invitations to wholeness. Dark things chase the light. Light things chase the dark. Balance brings us back to humble wholeness.

There are times when getting-to-wholeness involves a bit of crazy. The gray matter tosses us about a bit, for the sake of wholeness.

"Be silent and listen: have you recognized your madness and do you admit it? Have you noticed that all your foundations are completely mired in madness? Do you want to recognize your madness and welcome it in a friendly manner? You wanted to accept everything. So accept madness too. Let the light of your madness shine, and it will suddenly dawn on you. Madness is not to be despised and not to be feared, but instead you should give it life. .. indeed, madness is a special form of spirit...." (Carl Jung in <u>The Red Book</u>)

Far too often what we are doing along this healing journey is wishing we were not where we are, wishing we were better, wishing those things that drag us down simply did not exist. These parts of ourselves become the enemy, abandoned even. But if we are choosing to heal then we are impelled to befriend the enemy. We must in fact, let our suffering speak to us. We must bring home the abandoned ones. It is our job to seek out the ones we have forgotten, the ones we have tried to hide or get rid of in ourselves.

"Perhaps all the dragons in our lives are princesses who are waiting for us to act, just once, with beauty and courage. Perhaps everything that frightens us is, in its deepest essence... something helpless that wants our love." Rainer Maria Rilke

Artists often work intimately with what is known as negative space: the space around the main object in a painting or photo for example. But, like the words "black" and "shadow," *negative* here does not refer to bad or unwanted. Working with the negative space is as important if not MORE important for the success or wholeness of the finished piece. Some artists will make the seeming lines between the two distinct, others will let them overlap or seem soft and mingling (think realism versus impressionism for example), but even the distinct lines are dependent upon both "sides" of negative space, positive space, dark and light, shadow and awake. Some indigenous people speak of the dream as that place to charioscurify --living slightly in awake and slightly in sleep, slightly in the past and slightly in the future. It is an important dance.

In healing work, we accept our shadow and bring our abandoned bits of self, the "I don't like this about me" parts, home - as teachers. Teachers do not define us – they give us boosts forward by sharing their gifts. We can enlighten and complete them while they enlighten and complete us. If and when we cannot do this, or refuse to, then we end up going about making OTHERS the dark scary awful horrible shadow we think we need to get rid of. But what if we saw the OTHER enemy with the same compassion we embody toaccept the INNER so-called enemy?

"It is the enemy who can truly teach us to practice the virtues of compassion and tolerance." The Dalai Lama

If my enemy is not really my enemy, if the abandoned ones are sitting there waiting for me, if those I disagree with are a mirror of my shadow self, then I cannot think of them as "all bad." I cannot think of them as "black" as truly as I cannot look to any outside authority or myself as all "white."

Nothing is all bad or all good. Healing calls us to chiaroscurify in all things.

If instead we only see the enemy as the enemy, and not "like us," (a whole big gray mix of stuff) then we are stuck in dualism. We think a shadow is truly a solid thing and that black is black and white is white. This kind of thinking is not just scientifically erroneous, but psychologically and spiritually erroneous as well. Look to the world: this kind of thinking is hurtful to everyone. It makes some people bad and some people good. In the Western Christian world of 2018, it has caused a torrent of people proclaiming exclusion as the way to be. We are right. We are good. We have the answers. You and you and they, do not. My church is better than your church. My spirituality is better than your religion. My separation of church and state is better than your mixing of faith and actions. My color is lighter than yours. (etc. etc. etc.)

This is a time when more and more people are aware of the horrific effects of dualism. Black and white thinking and judging is not serving us personally or communally.

"Wetiko thrives off of polarization, separation. So if I see somebody who is embodying wetiko, and I recognize that we are living in a shared consciousness, then that person is really an embodied reflection of that sick part of me. Then you have cut through the separation, and you are actually engendering compassion – which is the energy that dispels Wetiko." (Paul Levy)

For me, these observed actions bring me to the study and living way of creative nonviolence and this connects me to an ongoing search for what "forgiveness" means for me. This is not an easy word for many, many, many survivors of trauma. Nonviolence is also not a term everyone is fond of or understands. Is it the same as passive, of pacifist? Is there no room for some kind of force? How violent is violent? Is it about actions, or words also? Aren't words also actions? WHY nonviolence? What does "love your enemies" really mean? Whole books, seminary papers, theses, Facebook rants… are written on one side or another of the question, "do we have to forgive to heal?" What does forgiveness really mean? Does it let perpetrators off the hook? Is it for their sake or for mine? Does it change anything or do any good? Is it just a show or a burden?

I have come to two overlapping conclusions so far. These are only mine. I mention them not as answers for anyone else, but as my sharing of where I am at right now.

I am committed to continuing research, study, prayer and living according to the tenets of nonviolence. For me this is as much (if not more) in words as in other outer actions. It is a recognition that all of us are broken in some way, and all of us are WHOLE as we let our light and dark sides search each other out, illumine each other, and grow. There are shadow things within me, semi-conscious and unconscious, which guide my thoughts and actions. I seek to understand them and let them help me awaken. I work hard at self-compassion as a form of non-violence. I also work at compassion as a form of outward nonviolence. The "enemy" (an old abuser, an institution, a politician etc. etc. etc.) mirrors me. They struggle with balance and wholeness. They have shadow parts of self, abandoned parts of self, unconscious parts of self – all guiding them, for better or worse. Sometimes compassion means I stay away and let them go on their own journey.

So, my personal FORM of forgiveness is a nonviolent stance towards the enemy and abandoned ones in others and in myself. I will speak up. I do not forget. I will act. I will NAME injustice and seek to love justly. AND, I will leave the door open that their hearts and minds might be moved to something new.

My inner abandoned parts may actually be hurt and scared little children who have things to learn and to teach me, if we work together. If I hold that hope for myself, I hold it for others as well. Forgiveness, for me, means that because of that hope I let you go upon your journey, enemy of mine. I will not hold you bound. I will not let my judgment or pain hold ME bound. Things like judgment are also held in the body. That tension and pain can hold me bound, keep me in pain. So consider freedom instead. Look for the stories of forgiveness when enemies have learned to work together or ever become life-long friends. There are options.

It is not easy, this "accept your shadow" and "dance in the balance" stuff. It is difficult work. It needs enough purpose to keep going. There is good purpose.

It is FAR EASIER to remain in black and white thinking where there is a right and wrong and where we feel some control. Gray has less control. Having to change is not about needing control. But this hard work is the path everywhere, the path to wholeness.

We are one ever-flowing body seeking an even larger wholeness and "the way you fall into wholeness is by suffering it." (Richard Rohr OFM) Perhaps we also fall into it by dancing the dance and practicing how to chiaroscurify all of life.

Affirmations:

I am whole.

I can welcome my abandoned parts, and those aspects of myself I do not like. I can bring them home and let them teach me.

I am not all good or all bad. I am not all black or all white. I am wholeness as a living force, ever growing, ever changing, ever flowing.

The shadow in me, and the shadow in others, is a source of light, a great awakener, for all.

What is true for me is true for all and I have compassion for us all.

I leave the door open.

Possible questions to ask:

If my experience of trauma and healing is much the same as the truth about shadows, what does that mean? Can I feel in my body the ability to chiaroscurify?

What do I think of as my shadows, the things I don't like about myself? If I asked the people who know me best, could they tell me more about what I deny, avoid, am afraid of in myself? Can I welcome them as if they were little children tugging at my sleeve? Can I throw light on them and see them newly? How do things transition and move in all those layers of gray in between? Am I a giant impressionist painting? Is it all good? Will all be well? Has my understanding of forgiveness changed? How do I define it? How do I do it?

Ideas for more on these themes:

-research nonviolence (for example the Metacenter.org, Walter Wink, Gandhi and the history of nonviolent movements around the world).

-google several sites about Ho'o pono pono.   -

-Look up the article written by Rev. Lynn James: "Forgiveness as an Act of Defiance," September 2014. **www.lynnjames.net** writings.

-pay attention to the physical shadow you cast, play with movement, take photos. It is not a scary thing. It isn't EVEN a thing, but a playing with differing degrees of light.

-talk to artists about the importance of negative space.

-read Richard Rohr's paper, "Creation as the Body of God."

-Revel in a large full color copy of the Red Book and Carl Jung's own journey with the shadow.

-research Taoism and all the applications of yin and yang. Come up with your own.

-talk to child parts of yourself you haven't talked to before or avoided. Adopt your lost children.

Creative nonviolence connection:

Leave the door open.

"Out beyond the ideas of wrongdoing and rightdoing there is a field. I will meet you there." Rumi

"To let ourselves feel anguish and disorientation as we open our awareness to global suffering is a part of our spiritual ripening. Mystics speak of the 'dark night of the soul.' Brave enough to let go of accustomed assurances and allow the old mental comforts and conformities to fall away, they stand naked to the unknown. They let processes which their minds could not encompass work through them. Out of darkness, the new is born."
(Joanna Macy)

THE SUN. Acrylic on canvas board. Painting by a 4 yr old friend.

To Become The Sun

What can it mean?

If my experience of trauma and healing and spirit is so much like the sun, then what does that mean for me? Can I feel it in my body somehow, observe that and learn from it? Can I let the sun's energy rest on my skin and penetrate, in light and in dark?

I assume that because the sun is at the center of our solar system, it has been the center of our thinking and our sense of meaning, forever. There are far too many possible ways to use the sun as a metaphor for trauma and healing and spirit. For now, I have chosen three themes: constant pulsing movement; continuous giving and relational truth; spiritual connection. Mostly I suggest some metaphors, discuss meaning, and ask questions. I would like the conversation to continue for a long, long time.

Movement:

In the sun's core there is constant action and reaction, continuous breaking down of one element into many particles, which then join up in new ways to form another element, slightly heavier. Mostly this goes on with hydrogen breaking down and helium being made. We call this nuclear fusion. When the hydrogen isotopes collide with each other it is said to be like cars smashing into each other at high speed, with tiny parts of cars flying all over the place. The 'crash' creates an enormous amount of energy and the tiny particles then fuse together as a new molecule, helium. There are so many tiny nuclear reactions happening inside the sun at any given time we don't even HAVE a number for them. The energy from each reaction then travels to the core of the sun, through other layers and finally to the exterior (photosphere) which we can see during the day from earth. That energy is mostly in the form of gamma-ray photons and neutrinos. Somehow the photons can bounce around at random for a million years, while the sun releases neutrinos towards earth on a regular basis. Once reaching the photosphere more chemical reactions occur and the energy is transmuted into warmth/heat and light. These pass through the outer layers of the sun's atmosphere and then move towards the earth. While it can take a million years for the energy of a single nuclear fusion to move from the core to the photosphere, once there it is said the heat and light reach the earth in about 8 minutes.

As the sun is the center of the universe, our hearts are the center of our being. That pulsing force keeps our body going. The core of the sun and the core of our being are made up of a constant experience of breaking down and joining up: collision, explosion, break-down, attraction and repulsion, change and integration (the making of something new.)

"If you're really listening, if you're awake to the poignant beauty and suffering of the world, your heart breaks regularly. In fact, your heart is made to break; its purpose is to burst open again and again and again so that it can hold evermore wonders."
(Andrew Harvey)

Quantum physics would suggest that the entire universe is creating by the same packet of energy repeating itself, the quantum wave. Much philosophy, psychology and theology would make the same suggestion about the human heart and the history of meaning: love. Trauma can feel as big and violent as a nuclear reaction. Healing can feel as new as each and every hydrogen molecule which fuels all life and growth on our planet and beyond. Put the two together in their constant movement and pattern and we are guided toward a description of the heart. Helioseizmologists suggest the sun's wave pulses like a heart and actually makes a pulsing sound.

    What is going on in the sun, goes on within us. Even when we are calm, we are made of movement and change. Our breathing, our heart, every synapse and neuron and atom of our being is breaking down and integrating again. We are a whirl of energy disconnecting and connecting again all the time. And all of it is for life. We "give off" warmth and share the life force with all. The more healing we do, the more this sharing is a gift, an act of love. We are the sun for each other, or can be. We resonate with the sun in the same way we can resonate with each other. Our entire being is meant to be a source of light and warmth.

Constant giving and relationship.

Energy. Warmth. Light.

That which enables life never stops.

Warmth and light are somewhat discernable and defined. The energy at their core is something bigger and faster than we grasp, and is in the place between. There is the core nucleus, the protons and neutrons, points on the paper. Then there is the whirling of energy signified by rounded petals sort of, which taken together make up everything we know as anything. There are many words for this energy found in traditions and cultures around the world.

"The word 'prana' coming from the root 'An,' to breathe, signifies not only human breath but the breath of the universe, the life force. It is thus similar to 'chi' in Taoism, 'ruach' in Judaism, and 'pneuma' in Greek thought. It is the tendency of the unmanifest to vibrate and take form." (from the Kaushitaki Upanishad)

Spirit. Word. Wakan Tanka. Christ Consciousness. Orgone Energy. Baraka. Holy Spirit. Magnetism. Ki. Archetype. Synchronicity. Lifeblood. Divine Spark. Wisdom. Word. Psyche. Effervescence. Luminosity. God. Goddess. Higher Power. The Force. Does it matter so much what we call it, or what word we choose to point towards it? Personally, I like the word Grace.

"And still, after all this time, the sun never says to the earth, 'you owe me.' Look what happens with a love like that; it lights up the whole sky." (Hafiz)

Metaphorically, the sun's energy is the life force, and all things move in relation to that life force, constantly. And because of all the inter-relations, the energy given off is giving –it turns into the warmth and the light we depend upon. It does not give off its energy into a void, but for life. In the same way, we do not do our healing work in a void, but for life. And life is about connection.

There are many healing modalities which aid us in making connections. We can always be about deepening our connection with our bodies, our inner being, with those close to us, with all of nature, with what we understand as our 'higher power', and importantly, with all of the parts-of-self that make us who we are.

Internal Family Systems (IFS) is a modality for therapy created by Richard Schwartz, PhD. It is a systems model which directly works with what is referred to as multiplicity of the mind. It is based on the premise that all of us have many parts, aspects of our wholeness which interact and react and break down and re-build constantly, as we grow and heal. The relationships between the parts are brought into the therapeutic space. Once some of this conscious process is engaged, the healing model allows for something new to be revealed: The core Self. IFS practitioners speak of qualities of the core self which they call the eight C's: compassion; creativity; courage; clarity; calmness; confidence; curiosity; connectedness. Besides all of our individual parts of self, this Core Self is always present and always undamaged. It carries a deep wisdom as to how to allow the parts to interact. It is the energy behind the quantum pattern of being whole. We are made up of all these parts-of-self, yet we are also MORE than the mere sum of our parts. There is wholeness, which is not a *thing* so much as an energy – like the life force, the constant pulsing life force within us and without.

IFS helps people to understand and work with the inner-relationships. The process is relational and the healing work impels us always towards more and more connection. Trauma occurs in relationships – healing does as well. The eight C's help to portray for us what healing relationships are about. Like energy, warmth and light, they come from the core self, they help to navigate all the parts work.

I think a drawing of the IFS model could resemble an atom. There is the Core Self, and then all the parts whirling about in constant acts of dis-integration and re-integration, and the energy involved is life-giving and a source for warmth and light and greater and greater capacity for connection. This atom-model is also akin to seeing the sun at the core of our universe.

All the planets whirl around the center, the Core which provides for life and "navigates" what goes on with all the other "parts" of the galaxy. Everything is connected.

Trauma is about LACK of connection. Healing is about connection – internally and externally. Connection is what all of nature is about, all the universe. When we heal and move into better and better relationships internally and externally, we are copying the universe.

"Quite a few years of my life have strengthened my conviction that each and every one's existence is deeply tied to that of others: life is not merely passing by, life is about interactions... happiness can only be discovered as a gift of harmony between the whole and each single component. Even science – and you know it better than I do – points to an understanding of reality as a place where every element connects and interacts with everything else.... "(Pope Francis defining solidarity, tenderness and hope in a world of struggle. Ted Talk April 2017)

How essential it is to be mindful of our relationships. Understanding how intensely the entire universe interacts is an insight which invites us to more mindfulness. It is a concept which frees us up from being alone (as we often are in times of suffering, hence we experience trauma). It invites and welcomes new and ever-more healing connectedness.

Neil DeGrasse Tyson speaks poetically and scientifically of how we are all made of the same stardust, *literally.* (google it.)

"Through new relational experience – with a lover, a friend, a therapist, a baby, a star, a deer, a mountain, the moon – love is hidden inside caverns of neural circuitry. It is the substance which forms the neurons and their substances, lighting up heart cells in a moment of connection. Each time you attune to another – or to the inner 'other' within you – a new world is born." (Matt Licatta, therapist, writer and retreat director on his blog, *A Healing Space – Reflections on Love and the Intimacy of Immediate Experience. March 2017)*

I appreciate very much Matt's mention of the deer, a star, a mountain and the moon. I would add all the metaphors in this book and every other possible experience with nature. We can and must in fact connect deeply with nature, and not be solely about the experience of humans as if we are NOT part of nature, or as if we are not LIKE all of nature. Nature teaches us what we are like. Deep connection through language (metaphor), emerging models of trauma healing, and physical experience in nature will help to heal us and the earth together. How nature works is how the universe works is how healing works. The "stuff" of creation is also the "stuff" of healing. Every thing and every experience and every one, belongs.

"At times I feel as if I am spread out over the landscape and inside things, and myself living in every tree, in the splashing of waves, in the clouds and animals that come and go, in the procession of seasons. There is nothing ... with which I am not linked." (Carl Jung)

Intentional connection with nature must become more and more a part of our culture – across the globe. We heal the earth, we heal ourselves. What words we choose to describe this experience, are important. Hafiz wrote that the words we use become the house we live in.

"As long as I live I'll hear waterfalls and birds and wings sing. I'll interpret the rocks, learn the language of the flood, storm, and the avalanche. I'll acquaint myself with the glaciers and wild gardens, get as near the heart of the world as I can." (John Muir)

This connection with the earth is not meant to be selfish. It is not simply that nature makes us feel better. This connection is meant to be mutual because we are part of nature, not separate. We cannot solve the problems in our hearts, or in the heart of the world, without true connection with nature. Is it any wonder that many spiritual traditions begin with myths of creation?

Spiritual Connections.

Spiritual truths being associated with the sun dates back to the beginning of humankind, I feel sure. Spiritual myths and legends and practices abound in all traditions and cultures.

"The sun, each second, transforms four million tons of itself into light... as each day the sun dies as the sun and is reborn as the vitality of the earth." (Brian Swimme)

For me, this metaphor hearkens to the Christian tradition. So, *To Become The Sun* is to know the vital energy within one's wholeness, to be willing to die and be reborn constantly, and to BE A SOURCE for the vitality of the earth. To become the sun is to be incarnated as the working of the universe and be a source for the energy, warmth and light that our wounded world needs.

Indeed, In <u>Hymn of the Universe,</u> Pierre Teilhard de Chardin uses nature metaphors to bridge his mystic heart with his scientific brain. Published in 1961, the book pushes for an intimate and spiritual connection with nature, using science. De Chardin's words are words for today:

"What must mark a Christian in the future is an unparalleled zeal for creation."

You don't have to be spiritual, or a Christian, to understand all the metaphors of connection, from nature, which help us to better understand trauma and healing.

Affirmations:

I am one with the light of creation whole sole (soul/heart) purpose love.

I have many parts, like all creation, interacting and patterning as I heal and grow.

I have a core self that sources warmth and light for me and others and all nature.

I am free of the shame of disintegration.

I allow the natural patterns of breaking down and coming together again throughout my life.

I am one with all nature. Nature is one with me.

My heart is like the heart of the sun.

I am made of stardust, the same stardust we are all made of.

Everything belongs.

I take care of the earth as she teaches me who I am.

Possible questions to ask:

If still I find that my experience of trauma, healing and spirit are so much the same as I understand the sun and its workings, what does that mean to me? Can I feel the different phases in my body, observe the breaking down, the coming together, the source of energy and light?

What more can I do to help heal the wounds of the environment? When I see litter on the ground, or when I view online images of plastic islands and animals dying from plastic in their stomachs or wrapped around them, do I feel it in MY body too? Do I truly relate to all of creation as Sacred? Holy? Part of my higher power? Part of me? Could I find a healer or therapist or shaman who would work with me in nature? What are all my parts – who are they? Do I hide them? Why? How can I better work all the parts of my Self, and gain deeper connection with my Core Self? How can I deepen my relationships with others? Do I truly understand how it is all connected?

Ideas for more on these themes:

-Pay attention to how birds tend to sit watching the sunrise and sunset from the tip top of trees.

-Find books and google website on eco-therapy and nature-based spiritual activities.

-Google the photography of Craig Burrows, who has created time-lapse images of light being given off by plants.

-Look up research on the Quantum Wave by people like Max Planck. Study Fractals.

-Find all you can about various myths of creation and the sacredness of life, and the sun in particular.

-Watch the online video by Bruce Lipton, "The Imaginal Cells in the Dying Caterpillar."

-Read John Muir and other naturalists.

-Pilgrimage to favorite places in nature and create new body-memories of connection. Do yoga outside. Dance in the woods. Hug trees. Read to a flower. Sing to your cat. Talk to your tomato plants. Explore new ways of connecting with nature and pay attention to the shifts in your body.

- Lay down on the earth and go barefoot – a lot.

-Tesla said that all the world is fueled by the eternal. What do you think he meant?

-Learn about IFS, the different parts you have, and your Self. (**www.selfleadership.org**)

-Read Soren Kierkegaard on the concept of grace.

-look up the myriad people coming up with new technologies to work against plastic waste, across the globe. Make it a spiritual quest – or not.

-meditate.

Non-violence connection:

Non-violence as a way of life, and non-violent actions, depend upon the butterfly effect, or the quantum wave. Consider how each thought, word and action affects all that is around you, and vis-versa: this is mindfulness. Nature teaches us this.

More on why I wrote this book.

I am interested in helping to shift the way we look at trauma and healing and spirit. I think many of the traditional ways in which we approach these fields can be re-imagined and expanded. I am not interested in negating the positive history, or the exciting present movements in all three areas. I simply want to add another perspective, primarily from my own experience. The following are things I believe which source the motivations for this book and experimenting with natural metaphors.

Trauma is the internal experience resulting when some external thing happens which hurts us in an overwhelming way: we do not have the resources inwardly or outwardly to repair the harm. The energies attached to the event stay stuck in the body, causing a myriad of physical symptoms, and these affect our mind and heart so intimately we also end up with symptomatic, limiting and stuck beliefs and practices.

The world we live in is full of suffering. The global media experience intensifies how much suffering and injustice exist and it is all but impossible to repair this harm to our spirit in an ongoing, every day or minute way without right supports. As whole communities we walk around with unresolved trauma to our bodies, minds, spirits and hearts (moral trauma). To say that all suffer trauma is true. The word is no longer limited only to those who have undergone child abuse or rape or war. It is a global phenomenon. To one degree or another, depending on our personal circumstances and supports, we all suffer post traumatic stress. Because of these facts, we all experience deep disconnection with our own bodies and spirits, with others, with the present moment, and with nature. Trauma is an every-day reality; an every-day experience of the internal world being disconnected because of so many external pains and horrors.

Healing is a process of repair. It is the careful and conscious, compassionate attention to the harm felt in our body, mind and spirit. It is a way of being which intentionally recognizes the harm, cares for it, and releases stuck energies so that body, mind and spirit are free to embrace original innocence and connection. We are created for connection and we are created innocent. We are created in the same way the universe was created and the patterns of the universe are alive in us. This means that healing is possible because the universe, all of nature as we know it, has inherent abilities to shift and change as necessary, to adapt and transform. Healing is about repairing the breach, filling the gap between me and myself, me and others, me and the present moment, me and the natural world.

One powerful way to approach trauma, healing and spirit is through our words. (The words we use become the house we live in. Hafiz) Metaphor is a way of using words to intermingle the different fields of trauma, healing and spirit. These things overlap in ways we cannot easily explain, cannot explain in clear, linear ways. Things which overlap and wrap around each other and move constantly, cannot be simply lain down in exact, static words. So, we use metaphor. Metaphor is about connection.

There are many books written, and people speaking, about the use of metaphor in the trauma-healing fields. This is good. My concern, however, and the motivation for the focus of this book, is about the KIND of metaphors often used, and the purpose/intention.

When applying metaphor to my own life of trauma and healing and spiritual work, I deeply want to use metaphors which inherently imply and declare things like resiliency, sustainability, courage, process, belonging, integration, transformation, connection. I also want to be able to come up with my OWN metaphors for my experience - *not just as an explanation so that someone else can grasp my experience* – but as a truth about my life that I am free to share.

A lot of common metaphors for trauma are neither of these things. How often do you hear people speaking of their trauma as a straightjacket or a curse? We talk of depression as a liquid seeping out of a closed box. We are the walking dead. We speak of anxiety as forever being hit with a cattle prod. Post-traumatic stress means we are broken, shattered, alone in a dark room without doors. We are swallowed up by grief. We are stuck in a glass bottle afraid to move because of shame. Rage is a grizzly clawing at our chest and we have no arms to stop what is happening. Despair is a wolf staring in our eyes while eating our heart. I could go on and on.

Perhaps at times these metaphors are helpful in conveying the pain involved. But to me, if these are the **only** or main words we are using, if these are the images we are imagining while talking about our LIFE and our real experience, they are not ultimately hopeful and not about connection. But I want hope! I need connection.

So here is my experiment. What if we put some intention into creating new metaphors for all these things we experience as trauma? What if we use natural, living metaphors instead of static harsh non-nature ones? Nature inherently embodies the goals of healing work: resiliency, process, transformation, freedom, agency, creativity, resonance, recovery, authentic power, cooperation and inter-connection, etc. Nature is all about connection, so using natural, living metaphors is a way of using our words to conjure up in the psyche and spirit, in the body and mind, all of the inherent awesome truths about nature and know they are in us.

And perhaps, if we connect more consciously with nature in this way, we can imagine feeling what nature feels and then experience more agency to take care of the environments which sustain us. We will grasp the truth of our human complicity in the changing climate threats. We will pick up litter in the park where we walk our dog. That is resonance. That is an effect of connection. We are not separate from nature in truth. We ARE nature. If we change our words and images through metaphor, we change the quality of our connections. We care more. We spend more time in body, mind and heart with what we care for and feel intertwined with.

So, what if my experience of trauma and my experience of healing is mountains, the way a pearl is made, an unfolding flower, stones, compost, waves, embers, shadows and the sun?

What if I claim my pain IS an earthquake or fire (instead of like a straightjacket) and then delve into the science of earthquakes and resonate with the entire process. What if my fibromyalgia is fire ants? What can I learn about such a keystone species that would help my sense of resiliency, agency, determination, power, ingenuity? What if my depression is a dessert? What can I learn about how deserts used to be oceans, and what the wild life really is like in the desert, and so on, which would help me to understand time and process, small victories and secret wellsprings to be found? Maybe my internal family system is an ant farm or beehive. My childhood dissociation is a murder of crows and we grieve like elephants grieve, hanging on to the bones of our ancestors.

Metaphors, like all words, are limited, but also powerful. Nature metaphors are more-true to what healing is actually all about and can only be helpful. I fully intend to continue this experiment for myself. How might my experience be so much like the life of a platypus? an earthworm? Moss on the north side of trees? etc. I hope to invite others to do the same as well. How does your sense of SELF change if you change your metaphors about your pain, your process, your healing and joys?

Throughout this book I added a lot of spiritual quotes and hints. My personal connection with nature does not allow me to deny a spiritual connection. I also added a non-violence connection. Again, this is because what I find in my resonance with nature is a non-violent way of being. These two things are not necessary in order to use nature metaphors for one's experience. They are just part of MY nature metaphors for MY experience. I am happy to share them with you. I look forward to others sharing with me.

Ani Rose   whalesunpress@gmail.com

Facebook page: To Become The Sun

**the authentic COLOR images for all the paintings in this book can be found on the FB page and the future website or blog.

Resources used in this book and further suggestions.

Muir, John. *Spiritual Writings: Selected with an Introduction by Tim Flinders.* New York; Orbis Books, 1970.

Renehan, Edward J. *John Burroughs: An American Naturalist.* New York: Black Dome Press, 1992.

Brown, Brene, Ph.D., L.M.S.W. *The Gifts of Imperfection: Let Go of Who You Think You're Supposed to Be and Embrace Who You Are.* Minnesota: Hazleden; 2010.   (See also her TED talks on vulnerability and shame.)

Griffin, Susan. *Woman and Nature: The Roaring Inside Her.* San Francisco: Sierra Club Books, 1978.

Tzu Lao. *Tao Teh Ching: translated by John C. H. Wu.* Massachusetts: Shambhala Publications, 1961.

Dallet, Janet O. *The Not-Yet-Transformed God: Depth Psychology and the Individual Religious Experience.* Maine: Nicolas-Hays, Inc, 1998.

Nabokov, Peter. *How the World Moves: Odyssey of an American Indian Family.* New York: Penguin Books, 2015.

Herrera, Hayden. *Listening to Stones: the Art and Life of Isamu Noguchi.* New York: Farrar, Straus, and Giroux, 2015.

Hanh, Thich Nhat. *The World We Have: A Buddhist Approach to Peace and Ecology.* California: Parallax press, 2008.

Morrell, Rima A., Ph.D. *Sacred Power of Huna: Spirituality and Shamanism in Hawai'i.* Vermont: Inner Traditions, 2005.

McKenna, Terence. *The Invisible Landscape: Mind, Hallucinogens and the I Ching.* New York: Harper Collins, 1993.

Koyzcan, Shane L. Spoken Word artist. His work can be found on poetry sites and recorded Ted talks online.

De Chardin, Pierre Teilhard. *Hymn of the Universe.* New York: Harper and Row, 1961.

Licatta, Matt, Ph. D. Blog: *A Healing Space: reflections on love, meaning, and the aliveness of immediate experience.* Matt is an author, retreat director and therapist.

Wei, Wu. *I Ching Life: Becoming Your Authentic Self. Living in Harmony with Universal Life.* California: Power Press, 2006.

Jung, Carl. *Man and His Symbols.* And, *The Red Book.*

Shearer, Alistair and Peter Russel (translators). *The Upanishads.* New York: Harper Colophon Books, 1978.

Dallet, Janet O. *When the Spirits Come Back.* Toronto, CA: Inner City Books, 1988.

Lorde, Audre. *Sister, Outsider.* California: Crossing Press, 1984.

Myss, Caroline, Ph.D. *Spiritual Madness: the Necessity of Meeting God in Darkness.* Audio CD: Sounds True, Inc,2002.

Levine, Peter. *Waking the Tiger; Healing Trauma.* California: North Atlantic Books, 1997.

Borysenko, Joan. *Fire in the Soul: a New Psychology of Spiritual Optimism.* New York: Time Warner Book Club, 1993.

Dallet, Janet O. *Saturday's Child: Encounters with the Dark Gods.* Toronto, CA: Inner City Books, 1991.

Fynn. *Mr. God, This is Anna.* New York: Ballantine Books, 1971.

Some, Malidome Patrice. *Ritual: Power, Healing and Community.* Oregon: Swan Raven and Company, 1993.

Brezny, Rob. *How the Whole World is Conspiring to Shower You with Blessings.* California: North Atlantic Books, 2005.

Levy, Paul. *Dispelling Wetiko: Breaking the Curse of Evil.* California: North Atlantic Books, 2013.

Macy, Joanna and Molly Young Brown. *Coming Back to Life: Practices to Reconnect Our Lives, Our World.* California: New Society Publishers, 1998.

Other quotes (E. Hemingway, Rainer Maria Rilke, Allen Watts, Walt Whitman, Rainer Maria Rilke, The Dalai Lama and Thomas Merton) came directly from Brainy Quotes online resource of famous quotes.

Most SUN facts were taken from the SOHO website: Solar and Heliospheric Observeratory of NASA.

See also:

Macy, Joanna. *Thinking Like a Mountain: Towards a Council of All Beings.* Philadelphia: New Society Publishers, 1988.

Bass, Diana Butler. *Grounded: Finding God in the World. A Spiritual Revolution.* New York: Harper Collins, 2015.

The Dalai Lama. *The Universe in a Single Atom: the Convergence of Sicience and Spirituality.* New York: Three Rivers Press, 2005.

White, Jonathon. *Talking on Water: Conversations about Nature and Creativity.* Texas: Trinity University Press, 2016. (This is a wonderful collection of interviews held on a boat with such figures as Ursula Le Guin, Gary Snyder, James Hillman, Matthew Fox and others. Creative, inspiring conversations over the ocean.)

Sheldrake, Rupert. *Science and Spiritual Practices.* Great Britain: Clays Ltd., 2017.

Arguelles, Jose and Miriam. *Mandala.* Boston and London: Shambala, 1995.

Whitman, Walt. *Leaves of Grass: The original 1855 Edition.* Kansas: Digireads.com, 2016.

Swimme, Brian. *The Hidden Heart of the Cosmos.* Online Video.

Wilson, Jim. *God's Cricket Chorus.* Online Video by Soulseekers Worldwide, 1992.

Cuppitt, Don. *Solar Ethics.* Self-published, 1995. "Solar Ethics means committing oneself to live as the sun lives, that is, to do what you were created to do without regard for recognition, permanence or reward."

Buzzel, Linda and Craig Chalquist, <u>Ecotherapy: Healing with Nature in Mind.</u> Sierra Club Books, San Francisco, California, 2009. (See also the website for the International Community for Ecopsychology, with their numerous resources/books.)

Plotkin, Bill, <u>Nature and the Human Soul: Cultivating Wholeness and Community in a Fragmented World.</u> New World Library, Novato, California, 2008

Richard Rohr's daily meditations /website (Center for Action and Contemplation in New Mexico)have had numerous articles about nature in 2018.

If you visit the fb page or website, or email me, please share my resources for me and others.

Ani Rose Whaleswan is an artist, writer, teacher, speaker and spiritual director, currently living in Colorado. Her work is both trauma-informed and eco-informed. She is primarily interested in re-visioning how we understand trauma and healing, and re-imagining how we speak of Spirit. She loves to work with others in advocacy, education, creative experiences and retreats (usually for women.) She is working with a somatic therapist a yoga teacher and others to develop retreat experiences which use this book and more natural metaphors. She is considering writing another book like this one, with all of the natural metaphors being about community and communication (internal and external); things like bees, murmurations, ant colonies, whale pods, elephant herds . . . slime mold! Contact her with thoughts and ideas!

In all areas of life, nature is our teacher for how to respond creatively and effectively. Climate anxiety? Other trauma? Spend time in nature and change your images and metaphors for what you are going through and who you are.

whalesunpress@gmail

Made in the USA
Middletown, DE
25 January 2020